SPANISH FLAVOURS

JOSÉ PIZARRO'S
SPANISH FLAVOURS

PHOTOGRAPHY BY EMMA LEE

KYLE BOOKS

* tomàquets
sucar, salsa o
gazpatxo
1 Kg: 2 €
A de Munt

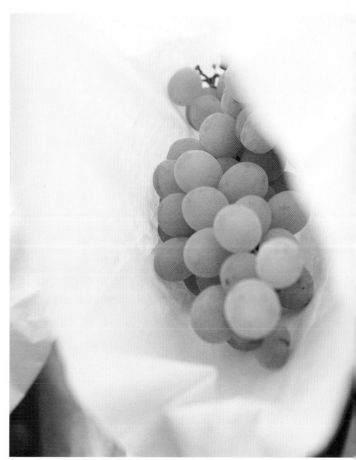

First published in Great Britain in 2012 by
Kyle Books
23 Howland Street
London, W1T 4AY
general.enquiries@kylebooks.com
www.kylebooks.com

ISBN: 978-0-85783-026-5

Text © 2012 José Pizarro
Photographs © 2012 Emma Lee
Design © 2012 Kyle Books

Editor: Sophie Allen
Designer: Peter Dawson, www.gradedesign.com
Designer's assistant: Louise Evans
Photographer: Emma Lee
Photographer's assistant: Rahel Weiss
Illustrator (page 17): Agata Frydrych
Props stylist: Lesley Dilcock
Food stylist: Debbie Major
Copy editor: Stephanie Evans
Production: Gemma John and Nic Jones

A Cataloguing In Publication record for this title is available from the British Library.

Printed in China by 1010 Printing International Ltd.

CONTENTS

INTRODUCTION

I was sitting in a bar in the port of San Sebastián in October 2010 during one of my many trips to Spain, looking for new ingredients and dishes for my new restaurants. I was enjoying a glass of txacoli, the local zesty dry white wine, while thinking about the theme for my new book. I churned over ideas about what it should be about: ingredients, the regions, the history, the producers and how I could bring all this together. I was getting more and more confused because there are just so many things to say about Spain. I think that Spain is like seventeen different countries all rolled into one. With the second glass of txacoli, things started to become clearer. It seemed logical to me that the regions of Spain, with their unique historical and climatic influences and their best-known ingredients, should form the basis of the book.

Spain is a very large country and so it seemed simplest just to divide it into the north, the east, the centre, the south and the islands.

The North – Galicia, Asturias, Cantabria, Basque Country, Rioja and Navarra – once one of the poorest regions, albeit very rich in gastronomic delights, is surrounded on two sides by the colder waters of the North Atlantic ocean and on the other, by the Cantabria sea. It has the greatest rainfall in Spain and is a mixture of mountains and green pastures, which influences not only the local ingredients but also the type of cuisine; seafood plays a great part, as does milk and therefore cheese, pork is invariably salted, the vegetables are robust, such as cabbage, potatoes and dried beans and there are chestnuts, and cider from the abundant apple trees. As a result the dishes are warming and filling yet inexpensive to produce and also highlight the two main occupations of the region, fishing and farming.

The East – Catalonia, Valencia and Murcia – runs along the Mediterranean shoreline, where the food appears to be almost more European and Mediterranean than Iberian. The ingredients here are influenced by the land and the sea: wild mushrooms and game from the mountains that border with France, vegetables from the fertile Ebro delta, fish and shellfish from the rocky shoreline, rice from the Albufera and citrus fruits from the warm fertile plains of the south.

The Centre – Aragón, Castile and León, Extremadura, Madrid and Castile La Mancha – is made up of the only landlocked regions of Spain, which are more arid and flat, with extremes of temperature between the summer and winter. Here there can be nine months of hell and 'a three-month freeze', as the locals put it. History plays an especially big part in the food of this region. The *conquistadores* who left Spain and discovered the new world brought back with them not only gold and silver but also potatoes, corn, tomatoes, pumpkins and red peppers from which the famous Spanish *pimentón* is made. The cork oak forests of the southern areas provide the perfect grazing for the Ibérico pig from which fresh pork and the more famous air-dried hams of Spain are produced, as well as chorizo, the traditional pork sausage flavoured with garlic and *pimentón*. Lentils and chickpeas are popular here and the saffron from the flat plains of La Mancha is considered to be the best in the world, along with Spain's most famous cheese, Manchego.

ESPAÑA

ASTURIA
CANTABRIA
Oviedo
Bilbao
BASQUE COUNTRY
NAVARA
Pamplona
FRANCIA

Coruña
GALICIA

la RIOJA

Saragossa
ARAGON

CATALONIA

Barcelona

Benavente
CASTILLE & LEON

MADRID
o Madrid

Toledo

EXTREMADUR
o Talaván

Badajoz

Valencia

Ibiza

Minorca
Majorca

ISLAS
BALEARES

CASTILLA LA MANCHA

MURCIA
Murcia

VALENCIA

o Serille
ANDALUCIA

Cadix

Portugal

Argelia

CANARIAS
Palma
Lanzarotte
Santa Cruz
La Gomera
Gran Canaria
fuerte ventura

The South – Andalusia – is greatly influenced not only by its proximity to two seas, the Atlantic ocean and the Mediterranean, but also the invasion of the Moors who ruled the region for over 800 years. They introduced a system of irrigation which helped to water what was previously a very dry area; they brought with them sun-loving fruits such as citrus fruits, strawberries, peaches, cherries, quince and dates, and vegetables such as aubergines and spinach; they introduced spices from the east into the local cuisine, and the tradition of sweet pastries and desserts. The coastline produces some of the best seafood in Spain: prawns, cuttlefish and anchovies from Huelva and tuna from Cadiz, octopus, sardines, red bream and red mullet. The food of this region goes with the climate, including as it does fresh (often chilled) dishes such as gazpacho and salads; and it was again the Moors who introduced the way of eating a collection of small dishes, known as mezze in the Middle East, which became tapas in my home country of Spain.

The Islands – the Balearics of **Majorca**, **Menorca** and **Ibiza** to the east of the mainland, and the volcanic Canary Islands of **La Palma**, **La Gomera**, **El Hierro**, **Gran Canaria**, **Ternerife**, **Fuerteventura** and **Lanzarote** far from the south of Spain, sitting in the South Atlantic, off the coast of the African Sahara desert – have developed their own styles of cooking, based largely around the crops they grow, the influences of nearby countries and again the human history. Although the islands of Spain are very different from each other, it seemed logical to group them together as 'the islands' because, being separated from the mainland, they are wonderfully distinct.

When you go through the book, you will see ingredients that you might think are situated in the wrong area. The reason they are in a particular section is because they are linked to my memories of travelling around Spain. This is not just about Spanish cuisine, but about Spanish ingredients and how I use them. I have showcased my favourite classic Spanish dishes, tweaked others to give my interpretation, but also I have used Spanish ingredients to create dishes that are not necessarily Spanish, but are still delicious. I always try to keep in mind what a home cook in a village in Spain would put together, using their local ingredients, as these combinations never fail to work – think of the seafood, game, rice and beans from the eastern regions that are combined to make delicious paellas and other rice dishes, or the warming winter stews from the northern regions that have had the same ingredients and cooking method for generations – this is what traditional Spanish cooking is about and I find it both humbling and inspiring.

I'm so lucky to be living in London and to be influenced by all the different cuisines that this city has. And of course, the British cuisine has had a great impact on me – the people involved, from the producers to the chefs, and the ingredients themselves. My cooking is all about simple yet stunning combinations that are easy to create at home. I hope you enjoy them!

THE NORTH

THE NORTH: INTRODUCTION

Northern Spain is famous for its gastronomy throughout the world. This vast land, bounded by mountains and seas, is rich in culinary resources and has a generations-old tradition of excellent food and drink. These mountains produce cheese, dairy and pork products that vie with the very finest of any other country. And I think the beef from the north is the best in Spain. Thriving fishing communities dot the long coastlines, landing fish and seafood of superlative quality on countless quaysides. Within this northern area, protected from external influence by its terrain, are distinct regions rightly proud of their profoundly separate identities and personalities, differences that are reinforced in the Basque Country and Galicia by maintaining their own languages.

When people ask me which part of Spain is my favourite, in food terms, I have to say the north. To me, culinary heaven would be to start eating in the Basque Country and to tour the entire north, ending in Galicia. San Sebastián has more Michelin-starred restaurants than anywhere in the world and I try to visit twice a year to experience as many of them as I can, but my favourite remains Arzak, both for its food and the brilliant foodie conversations I have with my friends Elena and her father Juan Mari Arzak. San Sebastián is so much more than Michelin stars and the New Basque Cuisine though – it is also about the pintxos bars and their simple, yet utterly delicious dishes that celebrate local seasonal ingredients.

Rioja, renowned for its wonderful wines, has also become a destination for culture tourists as well as gourmets. Beautiful boutique hotels, modern art and architecture sit happily with the centuries-old vineyards and bodegas. Lovers of good food must also try the chorizo from this region and, of course, cook it in Rioja wine. And the cauliflower from Calahorra is the most sublime you will ever try.

Navarra, one of the country's 'market gardens', produces outstanding artichokes, peas, broad beans and white asparagus, which we Spanish love. Don't be surprised to read on some tins of asparagus the word 'cojonudos', which literally means 'big balls'. This is a reference to a visit by King Carlos to a factory where he tried the white asparagus and proclaimed, 'Cojonudos!' meaning really delicious! The best way to eat asparagus is simply steamed or roasted with some very good mayonnaise or just olive oil and Ibérico ham. Navarra's other famous ingredient is the piquillo pepper, small, pointed and slightly piquant, which is used to flavour the lamb chilindróns of this region.

I remember Cantabria from childhood holidays with my family. One of my lasting memories is the first time I experienced that sweet smell of anchovies. Vast quantities of tuna, sardines and anchovies from the Bay of Biscay are prepared in the many family-owned seafood restaurants along the coast. Cantabria is also well known for its dairy products – *quesada pasiega*, a type of cheesecake, is a speciality of this region.

I go to Asturias as often as I can. This is where my friend Nacho Manzano has a great restaurant, Casa Marcial – you must order *arroz con pitu de caleya* and, of course the region's signature dish *fabada asturiana* (a pot of slow-cooked white beans, shoulder of pork or *lacón gallego*, chorizo, morcilla and often saffron). And don't forget to drink it with the local cider!

We end this culinary odyssey in Galicia, like the pilgrims who reach Santiago de Compostella. Galicia is famous for its fish and seafood from the Atlantic, including scallops, whose shell, the symbol of St James the Apostle, has been carried by pilgrims since the Middle Ages. The best-known white wine here is Albariño, but promise me you will try the Godello and finish your meal with a shot of orujo, a local digestif.

Artichoke, asparagus and fennel salad with crab mayonnaise

The best globe artichokes traditionally come from Navarra, the market garden of Spain, thanks to the fertile plains flanking the Ebro River. However, many people all over Spain now grow artichokes in their own gardens and I particularly enjoy those from my father's garden. His favourite way of eating them is either boiled then cut into wedges and sautéed in olive oil or simmered in a salt cod and potato stew. In this recipe, the fresh flavours from the green vegetables combine well with the sweetness of the crab. The white asparagus from this area are hugely popular in Spain – I like to eat them with some homemade mayonnaise.

Serves 4

4 large globe artichokes

juice of 1 lemon, plus 1 tablespoon

225g bunch of fine asparagus spears

175g fennel bulb

½ teaspoon Dijon mustard

3 tablespoons extra virgin olive oil

225g fresh white crab meat

2 tablespoons olive oil mayonnaise
   (see page 227)

1 tablespoon chopped fennel herb or
   flat-leaf parsley

sea salt and freshly ground black pepper

Working with one artichoke at a time, cut off the stalk and the dark green leaves from the base of the globe. Then cut off the top half with a large sharp knife and break away the remaining leaves until you reach the hairy choke at the centre. Slice the choke off the base with a small sharp knife and drop the base into a bowl of water acidulated with the juice of 1 lemon. Repeat with the rest of the artichokes.

Break off and discard the woody ends from each asparagus spear and cut the rest of the stalks into 5cm pieces. Drop them into a pan of boiling salted water and cook for 2 minutes until tender. Remove with a slotted spoon to a colander, refresh under cold water, then drain well on kitchen paper. Add the artichoke bases to the boiling water, bring back to the boil and cook for 6–7 minutes or until just tender. Drain, refresh with cold water and leave to drain well on kitchen paper.

Thinly shave the bulb fennel, on a mandolin or by hand, put into a bowl of iced water and leave for 5 minutes to crisp up. Meanwhile, whisk the remaining tablespoon of lemon juice with the Dijon mustard, then gradually whisk in the olive oil and some salt and pepper to taste. Drain the fennel and dry well (a salad spinner is ideal for this). Slice the artichoke bases across into thin slices and toss in a bowl with the asparagus, shaved fennel and lemon vinaigrette.

Put the crab meat into a bowl and gently stir in the mayonnaise, chopped fennel or parsley and seasoning to taste. Spoon some of the artichoke salad and crab mayonnaise onto each plate. Drizzle the remaining dressing from the artichokes over the top and around the outside of the plate, and serve.

Sautéed artichokes with cockles and jamón

The best cockles I've ever eaten were in the north of Spain, which is why I have put this recipe in the North chapter. The first time I encountered this dish was in La Taverna del Clinic in Barcelona with my friend Enric. I was instantly smitten by the earthy flavour imparted to the dish by the artichokes and the saltiness of the cockles. This is my version of that dish.

Serves 4

12 young globe artichokes

juice of 1½ large lemons, plus 2 teaspoons

1 teaspoon caster sugar

1kg cockles or small clams

4 tablespoons extra virgin olive oil

100g slice of Serrano ham or pancetta, cut into small dice

2 garlic cloves, finely chopped

1 tablespoon chopped flat-leaf parsley

sea salt and freshly ground black pepper

Working with one artichoke at a time, cut off the top half and then snap off the outer leaves until you reach the softer, pale pink and green leaves on the inside. Peel the stalk with a potato peeler, cut it into quarters lengthways and slice the hairy choke off the centre with a small sharp knife. Drop into a bowl of water acidulated with all but the 2 teaspoons of the lemon juice as you prepare each one. When they all prepared, drop them into boiling salted water with the sugar, bring back to the boil and cook for about 2–3 minutes until just tender. Drain, refresh under cold water and leave to drain well on kitchen paper.

Heat a large pan over a high heat. Add the cockles or clams and 150ml water, cover and cook over a high heat for about 30 seconds for cockles or 3 minutes for clams, uncovering and stirring once or twice, until they have all opened. Drain in a colander and, when they are cool enough to handle, remove the meat from the shells.

Heat 3 tablespoons of the olive oil in a frying pan over a high heat, add the artichoke pieces in a single layer and fry for 3–4 minutes, seasoning them as they cook, until they are lightly golden on each side. Lift out with a slotted spoon onto a plate. Add the remaining oil and the ham or pancetta to the pan and fry briefly for about 30 seconds until golden. Lower the heat, add the garlic and leave to sizzle for a few seconds. Add the artichokes and cockles or clams to the pan and toss over a medium heat to warm through. Add the remaining lemon juice, the parsley and some seasoning to taste, toss together briefly and serve.

Sardine empanada

A fish empanada has to be one of my all-time favourite snacks. Served warm from the oven with an ice-cold beer, a piece of one of these pies is heaven for me. Please use fresh sardines for this dish. Though it is also extremely good made with good-quality canned tuna steak or the tuna confit on page 158: simply drain the excess oil from the tuna, flake the fish into large pieces and scatter it over the sauce, with a few thinly sliced green olives or some shredded piquillo peppers if you wish. Eat on the day you make them. Another great and easy empanada is the recipe from my sister-in-law Maria José, which uses smoked salmon, onion and bacon.

Makes 10–12 pieces

For the dough
125ml milk

½ teaspoon caster sugar

2 teaspoons fast-action dried yeast

1 medium egg

25g butter, melted

275g plain flour, plus extra for dusting

1 teaspoon salt

beaten egg, for glazing

For the filling
6 tablespoons olive oil, plus extra for greasing

3 large onions, halved and thinly sliced

3 garlic cloves, crushed

400g vine-ripened tomatoes, skinned and chopped

½ teaspoon sugar

600g small fresh sardines

sea salt and freshly ground black pepper

To make the dough, warm the milk slightly in a small pan. Tip into a jug, whisk in the sugar and yeast and set aside somewhere warm for 15 minutes until foamy. Whisk in the egg and melted butter. Sift the flour and salt into a bowl, add the yeasty milk mixture and gradually blend the two together to form a soft dough. Tip out onto a lightly floured surface and knead until smooth. Put the dough into a clean bowl, cover with clingfilm and leave in a warm place for about 1 hour until doubled in size.

Meanwhile, make the filling. Heat the olive oil in a frying pan, add the onions and garlic, cover and leave to cook gently, stirring now and then, for 15 minutes until the onions are very soft and slightly caramelised. Add the tomatoes and sugar and simmer for 20–25 minutes until the mixture has reduced and thickened. Season to taste and set aside to cool.

Next, prepare the sardines. Gut them if necessary, then rinse them under the cold tap, rubbing off their scales with your thumb and snipping off the fins. Working with one fish at a time, cut off the head and slit open the belly cavity down to the tail. Open the fish out flat and place it skin-side up on a board. Press firmly along the backbone of the fish with the heel of your hand, then turn it over and pull out the backbone, cutting away the tail and any remaining bone. Check the fish fillet for any stray bones and remove them, then season on both sides with salt and pepper.

Preheat the oven to 200°C/gas mark 6. Lightly oil a 21 x 30cm shallow rectangular baking tray. Punch down the bread dough, turn it out again onto a lightly floured work surface and knead until smooth. Then cut it in two, making one piece slightly larger than the other (approx. 275g). Roll out the larger piece thinly and use to line the base and sides of the prepared tin, leaving the edges overhanging slightly.

Spread half of the onion and tomato sauce over the dough and arrange the opened-out sardines in a single layer on top. Cover with the remaining sauce. Roll out the second piece of dough to the same size as the baking tray and lay it on the filling. Brush the top with beaten egg, then fold the overhanging dough back over the top of the pie and press the edges together well to form a good seal. Pierce the top of the dough here and there with a fork to allow the steam to escape and bake for 30 minutes until crisp and golden brown. Remove from the oven and leave to cool in the tin on a wire rack. Cut lengthways in half and then across to give 10–12 pieces. Serve slightly warm or at room temperature.

Roasted red pepper and anchovy salad on roasted garlic toasts

The red peppers in Spain are outstanding and there is almost nothing better than peppers roasted in a proper wood-fired oven, a service that during my childhood was provided by the village baker. I'll always remember the aroma that filled the house when my mother returned from the baker's bearing a large tray of these wonderful vegetables. The combination of sweet roasted red peppers and salty anchovies is always a winner. This can be served as a tapas, as the larger Basque-style pintxos or even as a light lunch with a dressed green salad and a poached egg. If you're in a hurry, instead of roasting the red peppers, use a jar/tin of piquillo peppers, which are already roasted and skinned and have a great smoky flavour.

Serves 4

2 large heads of garlic, unpeeled, plus 1 fat
  clove, finely chopped

4 large thyme sprigs

1½ tablespoons extra virgin olive oil

4 large red peppers

2 tablespoons sherry vinegar

8 small slices of rustic white bread, about
  1cm thick

16 good-quality anchovy fillets in olive oil,
  drained

sea salt and freshly ground black pepper

Preheat the oven to 200°C/gas mark 6. Remove the outer papery skin from each head of garlic and take a thin slice off the top of each one to expose the cloves. Tear off a large square of foil, place the heads of garlic in the centre, add 2 of the thyme sprigs, drizzle each head with 1 teaspoon of the olive oil and sprinkle with a little salt. Wrap securely in the foil, place in a small roasting tin along with the peppers and roast on the top shelf of the oven for 20–30 minutes, turning the peppers once or twice until the skins have blackened in places. Remove the peppers from the tin, drop them into a plastic bag and leave until cool enough to handle. Return the garlic parcels to the oven and roast for a further 35 minutes, or until the cloves feel very soft when pressed.

Meanwhile, slit open the peppers, working over a bowl so that you catch all the juices, and remove and discard the stalks, seeds and skin. Tear the flesh into 1cm-wide strips and add to the bowl of juices with the chopped garlic clove, vinegar, the remaining thyme leaves and the rest of the olive oil. Stir well together.

Remove the garlic from the oven and set the parcel aside. Toast the slices of bread. (I like to put mine on the bars of a preheated cast-iron ridged griddle long enough to give the bread a slightly smoky taste, then finish it off in the toaster.) Unwrap the roasted garlic, squeeze some of the purée from each clove and spread it onto the toast while both are still hot. Sprinkle with a few sea salt flakes and some black pepper. Season the pepper strips with a little salt to taste and spoon onto the garlic toast. Garnish each slice with the anchovy fillets, drizzle over some of the pepper juices and serve while the toast is still crisp.

Griddled scallops with cauliflower purée and chorizo oil

The north-western region of Galicia is bordered on two sides by the Atlantic ocean and so it is not surprising that the cuisine of the area is greatly influenced by the sea. The Rias Bajas provide the perfect conditions for farming scallops and produce some of the highest-quality scallops in the world. The scallop shell is also the symbol of the town of Santiago de Compostella, the destination of pilgrims from around the world. Every year I promise myself I will make the effort to do the walk, but, as with the London marathon, I never quite get around to doing it! This dish is not traditional in the area, and some people might think it more French than Spanish, but I love the combination of flavours – the cauliflower and the spicy chorizo go so well with the sweetness of the caramelised scallops. You must try the cauliflower from Calahorra once in your life as they have an exceptional, sweet flavour.

Serves 4

600ml whole milk

300g cauliflower florets (about ½ medium cauliflower)

3 tablespoons extra virgin olive oil

50g cooking chorizo sausage, skinned and finely chopped

1 teaspoon sherry vinegar

1 teaspoon chopped flat-leaf parsley

12 large prepared scallops

sea salt and freshly ground white pepper

Bring the milk to the boil in a large pan. Add the cauliflower florets and 1 teaspoon of salt, return to the boil and cook for 7 minutes until tender. Drain well, reserving the milk. Put the cauliflower into a food processor with 3 tablespoons of the milk and 2 teaspoons of the oil and blend to a smooth purée. Season to taste with salt and pepper, transfer to a small pan and set aside over a low heat to warm through.

Heat 4 teaspoons of olive oil in a small frying pan over a medium heat. Add the chopped chorizo and fry it gently for 1 minute until just golden brown. Stir in the vinegar, parsley and a pinch of sea salt. Keep warm.

Heat a non-stick frying pan over a high heat. Rub the scallops with the remaining oil, add them to the pan and sear for 2 minutes on each side, seasoning them as they cook.

To serve, spoon some of the cauliflower purée onto 4 warmed plates and arrange the scallops alongside. Spoon over some of the chorizo oil and serve.

Seared scallops and black pudding on crisp potatoes with romesco sauce

To cook and eat a truly fresh scallop is one of the most wonderful culinary experiences imaginable. Try to buy scallops that are freshly opened and sold on the shell, with their corals still attached. They then caramelise beautifully. Don't buy scallops in plastic containers as they may be three weeks old.

Serves 4

1 quantity Romesco Sauce (see page 228)

500g small, waxy potatoes, peeled and cut into 5–6mm-thick slices

2–3 tablespoons extra virgin olive oil

leaves from 1 thyme sprig

2 x 100g smoked morcilla or 200g piece of black pudding, cut into 5–6mm-thick slices

12 large prepared scallops

sea salt and freshly ground black pepper

Make the romesco sauce and chill. Put the sliced potatoes into a pan of cold, salted water, bring to the boil and simmer for 5 minutes or until just tender. Drain well, leave until the steam has died down and then transfer them to a bowl and toss with 1 tablespoon of the oil, the thyme leaves and some salt and pepper. Preheat the oven to 170°C/gas mark 3.

Heat a ridged cast-iron griddle over a high heat. Lower the heat to medium, add half the potato slices in one layer and griddle for about 3 minutes on each side until crisp and golden. Lift them onto a baking tray and put in the oven to keep hot. Repeat with the remaining potatoes.

Rub the scallops with a little oil. Heat 2 large non-stick frying pans over a high heat and, as soon as they are hot, add the scallops to one pan and sear them for 2 minutes on each side, seasoning them as they cook. In the other frying pan, add 1 tablespoon of the oil and the morcilla/black pudding and fry for 1 minute on each side. Remove both to a plate. To serve, overlap the crisp potatoes in the centre of each of 4 warmed plates and arrange the scallops and black pudding on top. Spoon some romesco sauce to one side of the plate and serve.

Griddled octopus with olive oil mash

I may be biased but I think the best octopus in the world comes from Galicia and Spain's northern coastline. I think it has something to do with the cold waters there and possibly the local species. Octopus is firm, white and meaty with an almost gelatinous texture, which becomes meltingly tender on cooking. However, I like to cook it so that it remains a little firmer than is usual in Spain. The recipe only uses half the octopus, so use the other half for the recipe overleaf.

Serves 4

1 large onion, halved
2 large carrots, sliced
4 bay leaves
½ teaspoon black peppercorns
1 x 1.25kg frozen Spanish octopus, defrosted overnight
5 tablespoons extra virgin olive oil
3 garlic cloves, thinly sliced
1 teaspoon sweet *pimentón*
1 teaspoon red wine vinegar
sea salt and freshly ground black pepper

For the olive oil mash

900g floury potatoes, such as Maris Piper
4 garlic cloves, peeled but left whole
1 bay leaf
6 tablespoons extra virgin olive oil

Bring 8 litres of water to the boil in a large pan with the onion, carrots, bay leaves and peppercorns. Holding the head of the octopus between 2 forks, dunk it into the hot water, leave it for a few seconds, then lift it out and bring the water back to the boil. Dunk it once more and remove, bring the water back to the boil, return the octopus to the pan and make sure it is fully submerged. Cover and leave to simmer for 50 minutes –1 hour or until tender. If a skewer inserted into the thickest part of the tentacle goes in easily, it is done. Lift out the octopus and leave until cool enough to handle, then cut it in half through the head (and freeze one half).

Shortly before the octopus is ready, make the mashed potatoes. Peel the potatoes and cut them into small chunks. Put into a pan of well-salted water with the garlic cloves, bay leaf and 2 tablespoons of the oil. Bring to the boil and simmer for 15–20 minutes until the potatoes are tender.

Remove the octopus from the pan and, when it is cool enough to handle, cut the tentacles away from the head, separate them and then cut the head in half. (Freeze half of the octopus for another dish.) Put the remaining pieces onto a lightly oiled baking tray and brush with 1 tablespoon of the oil.

Once the potatoes are cooked, drain them through a colander set over a bowl to collect the cooking liquid. Remove and discard the garlic and the bay leaf, return the potatoes to the pan and mash until smooth. Skim the oil from the surface of the cooking water and stir into the potatoes with the remaining oil, some seasoning to taste and enough of the cooking liquid to give you a smooth, creamy mash. Cover and keep warm over a low heat.

Heat a ridged cast-iron griddle over a high heat until smoking, then reduce the heat to medium. Brush it with a little oil, add the octopus pieces and griddle them for 2 minutes on each side until lightly golden. Meanwhile, put the remaining oil into a small pan with the sliced garlic. Place over a medium-low heat and as soon as the garlic is sizzling and has lightly coloured, remove from the heat and add the *pimentón* and vinegar.

Spoon the mashed potatoes onto 4 warmed plates and top with the grilled octopus. Spoon over some of the garlic and *pimentón* oil, scatter with a little sea salt and serve.

Salpicón de mariscos

Salpicón, a fish and vegetable salad dressed with vinegar and olive oil, is found in tapas bars throughout the north. The choice of seafood is up to you, but for me the combination should always include prawns, octopus and mussels. It's not very common to use coriander, but it goes so well in this salad. This recipe makes a lot, so serve it up when you're entertaining. You can keep it marinated in the vinaigrette for the next day – just add the coriander at the last minute. Dunking the octopus prevents the tentacles from twisting together and the pink skin from tearing. This recipe uses only half the octopus, so freeze the other half for another dish (see page 33).

Serves 10–12

1 large onion, halved
2 large carrots, sliced
4 bay leaves
½ teaspoon black peppercorns
1 x 1.25kg frozen Spanish octopus, defrosted overnight
150ml extra virgin olive oil
400g (approx 14) large raw unpeeled prawns
12–16 razor clams, depending on their size
250g prepared squid
½ teaspoon crushed dried chillies
3 garlic cloves, finely chopped
500g large mussels, cleaned
finely grated zest of 1 small lemon and 3 tablespoons lemon juice
1 medium-hot red chilli, deseeded and finely chopped
1 small red onion, halved and thinly sliced
2 continental salad onions, thinly sliced
½ large red romano pepper, thinly sliced
20g bunch of coriander, roughly chopped
sea salt and freshly ground black pepper

Bring 8 litres of water to the boil in a large pan with the onion, carrots, bay leaves and peppercorns. Holding the head of the octopus between 2 forks, dunk it into the hot water, leave it for a few seconds, then lift it out and bring the water back to the boil. Dunk it once more and remove, bring the water back to the boil, return the octopus to the pan and make sure it is fully submerged. Cover and leave to simmer for 50 minutes –1 hour or until tender. If a skewer inserted into the thickest part of the tentacle goes in easily, it is done. Lift out the octopus and leave until cool enough to handle, then cut it in half through the head (and freeze one half).

Preheat the grill to high. Cut the tentacles from the head and separate them. Put onto a baking tray and brush with a little oil. Grill for 2 minutes on each side until lightly golden. Remove and leave to cool, then cut the tentacles on the diagonal into thin slices and the head into similar-sized pieces. Heat 1 tablespoon of the oil in a large frying pan over a medium-high heat, add the prawns and fry for 1 minute on each side until cooked through. Leave to cool, then peel, discarding the heads and shells, and cut them in half lengthways and then in half again across each piece.

Return the frying pan to a high heat. Add another 2 tablespoons of oil and half the razor clams, hinge-side down. As soon as they have opened, turn them over and cook for about 1 minute until lightly browned and cooked through. Remove and repeat with the remaining clams. Leave them to go cold, then remove the meat from the shells and cut each one into 3 pieces.

Slice the squid pouches across into rings and each bunch of tentacles in half if large. Heat another tablespoon of oil in the frying pan and add the squid and stir-fry for 2 minutes until cooked through and lightly browned, adding the crushed dried chillies, half the chopped garlic and some seasoning after about 1 minute. Spoon onto a plate and allow to cool.

For the mussels, heat a large saucepan over a high heat. Add the mussels and 4 tablespoons water, cover and cook for 2–3 minutes, shaking the pan now and then until they have all just opened. Drain and leave until cool enough to handle. Remove the meat from the shells.

Whisk the remaining oil and lemon juice together with the lemon zest, chopped chilli and remaining chopped garlic and season to taste. Mix the seafood together in a bowl with the red onion and romano pepper, then stir in the dressing. Just before serving, stir in the coriander and a little more seasoning to taste. Serve at room temperature.

Crab and prawn croquetas

In my bar 'José' and restaurant 'Pizarro', we love to change the *croquetas* recipe every day because we have so many regulars. The most popular used to be the Ibérico ham, until the crab and basil *croquetas* arrived – this recipe is the latest addition to the menu, with some prawns to add flavour and texture.

Serves 6–8 (makes approx. 35)

500ml whole milk
150ml chicken or vegetable stock
85g butter
115g plain flour
125g fresh white crab meat
100g cooked peeled prawns, finely chopped
1 tablespoon chopped flat-leaf parsley
2 large free-range eggs, beaten
200g breadcrumbs, made from stale, crustless white bread
olive oil, for deep-frying
salt and freshly ground white pepper

Put the milk and stock in a saucepan and bring to the boil. Melt the butter in another pan over a low heat, stir in the flour and cook gently, breaking up the mixture with a wooden spoon as it cooks, for 5 minutes, without letting it brown.

Very gradually beat in the milk and stock, beating really well between each addition, so that the mixture becomes silky smooth. Increase the heat very slightly and cook gently, stirring constantly, for 5–7 minutes, to cook out the flour.

Remove the pan from the heat and stir in the crab meat, prawns, parsley, plenty of salt and a little white pepper to taste. Transfer the mixture to a shallow dish, spread out in an even layer and press a sheet of clingfilm onto the surface. Allow to cool, then chill for 2 hours or overnight.

Put the beaten eggs and breadcrumbs into separate, shallow dishes. Lightly oil your palms and roll 1½-tablespoons (30g portions) of the chilled mixture into balls and then form into zeppelin-shaped barrels. You should make about 35. Refrigerate again for 15–30 minutes.

Heat some oil for deep-frying to 190°C. Dip the *croquetas* 4–5 at a time into the beaten egg and then the breadcrumbs and deep-fry for 2 minutes until crisp and lightly golden. Transfer to drain briefly on plenty of kitchen paper while you cook the rest. Serve hot.

Salmon en papillote on spinach with warm tomato and anchovy dressing

Cooking *en papillote* (in a paper parcel) is a perfect way to cook fish, ensuring it stays beautifully moist. I love to serve it with new potatoes. Try this dish with sea bream too.

Serves 4

4 tablespoons olive oil, plus extra
  for brushing and drizzling

leaves from 4 thyme sprigs

4 garlic cloves, thinly sliced

4 x 175–200g pieces of thick salmon or
  sea trout fillet, unskinned

500g baby leaf spinach, washed

sea salt and freshly ground black pepper

For the tomato and anchovy dressing

6 tablespoons extra virgin olive oil

2 tablespoons lemon juice

1 large vine-ripened tomato, skinned,
  deseeded and cut into small dice

3 anchovy fillets in oil, drained and thinly sliced

1 garlic clove, finely chopped

2 teaspoons small capers, drained and rinsed

2 teaspoons chopped flat-leaf parsley

Preheat the oven to 240°C/gas mark 9. Cut out 4 squares of foil and 4 of greaseproof paper, each 38 x 38cm. Put the foil squares on top of the paper ones, fold in half, then open up again and brush the centres with olive oil. Scatter the thyme leaves and garlic slices to one side of the crease of each one. Season the pieces of fish on both sides with salt and pepper, place on top of the thyme and garlic and drizzle 1 teaspoon of the oil over each piece of fish. Bring the other side of the square over the top of the fish so that the edges meet, then seal by folding over about 1cm of the edge, about 4cm at a time. Work your way all around the edge to make a semi-circular, airtight parcel. Put the parcels onto a baking sheet and bake for 8 minutes.

Meanwhile, for the dressing, put the oil, lemon juice, tomato, anchovies, garlic, capers and some sea salt and pepper to taste into a small pan.

Shortly before the fish is cooked, heat 2 tablespoons of the oil in a large pan. Add the spinach, a large handful at a time, stirring until it just begins to wilt before adding another handful. When all the spinach has wilted down, tip into a colander, gently press out the excess liquid, then return to the pan with the remaining oil and some seasoning and stir briefly to heat through. Place the pan of dressing over a low heat just to warm through.

Remove the parcels from the oven and slit them open with a sharp knife. Spoon the spinach into the centre of 4 warmed plates and place a piece of fish on top. Stir the parsley into the vinaigrette, spoon it over and around each portion and serve.

Pan-fried sea trout with sautéed summer vegetables

This is one of my favourite supper dishes. I can't wait for the first sea trout to appear at the local fishmongers. Although sea trout is rarely seen in Spain, salmon, which is caught regularly in the rivers of Asturias and Cantabria, makes a perfect alternative.

Serves 4

400g podded broad beans
8 baby carrots, halved lengthways
100g fine green beans, halved
20 asparagus tips, halved lengthways
3½ tablespoons olive oil
50g shallots, thinly sliced
2 garlic cloves, thinly sliced
4 x 175–200g pieces of thick, unskinned sea trout fillet
2 tablespoons chopped tarragon
sea salt and freshly ground black pepper

Bring a large pan of salted water to the boil. Add the broad beans, cook for 4 minutes, then remove with a slotted spoon and drop into a bowl of ice-cold water. Add the carrots to the boiling water with the green beans and cook for 2 minutes. Drop in the asparagus tips and cook for a further 2 minutes, then drain and add to the bowl of iced water. When they are cold, drain and dry well on kitchen paper. Skin the broad beans.

Heat 2 tablespoons of the olive oil in a large frying pan, add the shallots and garlic and cook gently until soft but not brown. Set aside.

Rub the sea trout with a little olive oil and season. Heat an ovenproof frying pan over a medium heat, add ½ tablespoon of the oil, then the sea trout, skin-side down, and fry gently for 4–5 minutes until the skin is crisp and golden. Carefully flip the pieces over and cook for a further 2 minutes. Set aside. The fish will continue to cook in the heat of the pan.

Heat another frying pan over a medium heat, add the remaining oil and the vegetables and toss together gently until heated through. Add the chopped tarragon and a little seasoning. Spoon the vegetables onto warmed plates, put the pieces of fish on top and serve.

Grilled cod with broad bean and mint purée and pancetta

It is quite rare to see fresh cod in Spain, but since I moved to the UK, I love tucking in to fish and chips now and then, with mushy peas. This dish is based on similar flavours, but instead of dried peas uses broad beans flavoured with a little mint, and has the addition of crisp, salty pancetta.

Serves 4

4 x 175–200g pieces thick, unskinned cod fillet

12 thin slices of pancetta or smoked bacon

salt and freshly ground black pepper

For the broad bean purée

4 tablespoons extra virgin olive oil, plus extra for drizzling

75g shallots, finely chopped

2 garlic cloves, crushed

600g broad beans, podded

2 tablespoons chopped mint

Heat 2 tablespoons of the oil in a small pan. Add the shallots and garlic and cook gently for 5 minutes until soft but not browned.

Preheat the grill to high. Drop the beans into a pan of well-salted boiling water and cook for 3 minutes or until tender. Drain well, remove the skins and then tip into a food processor and add a tablespoon of the olive oil, the cooked shallots and garlic, and the mint. Process until smooth, then transfer to a small pan and set aside.

Rub the pieces of cod with a little of the remaining olive oil and season with salt and pepper. Place skin-side up on a lightly oiled baking tray or the rack of the grill pan and grill for 6–8 minutes until just cooked through.

Just before the cod is ready, reheat the bean purée and season. Heat a large non-stick frying pan over a medium-high heat. Add 1 teaspoon of the oil and the slices of pancetta, side by side, and fry for 1 minute on each side until crisp and golden. Lift onto kitchen paper to drain. Spoon the bean purée onto warmed plates and place the cod on top, skin-side up. Rest the pancetta up against the cod, drizzle with a little olive oil, add a sprinkling of sea salt and a little crushed black pepper, and serve.

Pan-fried hake with cockles, asparagus, peas and mint

I cannot understand why the British do not love hake as much as the Spanish do. I remember during a visit to Padstow, to my friend Rick Stein's seafood restaurant, seeing a stream of lorries pulling away from the quayside, laden with crates of freshly caught hake, all bound for Spain. A similar dish is very popular in the North, using clams and parsley instead of cockles and mint, but this is my interpretation.

Serves 4

200g fine asparagus tips, cut into 2.5cm lengths
150g petits pois, freshly podded or frozen
3–4 tablespoons olive oil
90g shallots, finely chopped
3 garlic cloves, finely chopped
4 x 200g pieces of thick, unskinned hake fillet
500g cockles, cleaned
120ml fish or chicken stock
½ tablespoon chopped parsley
½ tablespoon chopped mint
sea salt and freshly ground black pepper

Drop the asparagus into a pan of boiling salted water and cook for 1½ minutes. Add the peas, cook for another 30 seconds or so until both the vegetables are just tender, then drain. Refresh under cold water and set aside.

Heat 1½ tablespoons of the oil in a large saucepan, add the shallots and garlic and cook gently for 4–5 minutes until very soft but not browned. Remove from the heat.

Rub the outside of the fish steaks generously with oil and season with salt and pepper. Heat a non-stick frying pan over a medium-high heat, add the hake skin-side down and fry for 2½ minutes or until the skin is crisp and golden. Turn the fish over, lower the heat slightly, and continue to fry for 4 minutes until cooked through.

Meanwhile, return the pan of softened shallots and garlic to a high heat and, as soon as it is hot, add the cockles and fish or chicken stock, cover and cook, shaking the pan now and then, for 2–3 minutes until the cockles have opened. Uncover and stir in the asparagus, peas, parsley, mint and some seasoning to taste.

Lift each piece of hake into the base of 4 large warmed soup plates, spoon some of the cockle mixture over and around the fish together with the juices, and serve.

Bacalao à la romana with anchovies and a green salad

For good *bacalao* (salt cod) the fish should be white, not at all grey or yellow, and smell sweetly of the sea even though it will have been out of the water for a long time. When I want to serve *bacalao* as a main course I prefer to use a cut called *lomo*, which are square-shaped portion-sized pieces of fish cut from the thicker end of the fillet, but for fritters, for example, where the fish is flaked into small pieces, the tail end cut is fine. Make sure that you soak it for just long enough to get rid of the excess salt but not for so long that it loses its characteristic taste.

Serves 4

4 x 150g pieces of thick *bacalao* (salt cod)
1 large soft lettuce
olive oil, for shallow-frying
plain flour, for coating
2 large free-range eggs, beaten
large pinch of sweet *pimentón*, to garnish
sea salt and freshly ground black pepper
8 good-quality anchovy fillets in olive oil, to serve

For the anchovy vinaigrette

2 good-quality anchovy fillets in olive oil, drained
1 tablespoon sherry vinegar
4 tablespoons extra virgin olive oil

Knock the excess salt off the cod and place it, skin-side up, in a bowl. Cover with plenty of cold water and leave to soak for 24 hours, changing the water every 6 hours or so. After this time, take a small piece of fish from the thickest part and taste it. If it doesn't taste too salty, it's ready to use, but remember, salt cod needs to be a little bit salty and also it will taste slightly more salty once it is cooked.

Drain the pieces of salt cod and leave them to dry well on plenty of kitchen paper. It is important to get rid of all the water, so press down lightly on the top of each piece to help remove any excess.

For the salad, remove and discard the outer leaves from the lettuce and break the rest into separate leaves. Wash and dry well and put into a large salad bowl.

To make the anchovy vinaigrette, put the anchovy fillets into a mortar or a small bowl and pound to a paste. Stir in the vinegar, gradually whisk in the extra virgin olive oil and season to taste with salt and pepper.

Pour 1cm of olive oil in a large non-stick frying pan, place over a medium heat until approximately 170°C (use a cooking thermometer). Coat the pieces of salt cod in flour, knock off the excess and then coat well in the beaten egg. Lower into the hot oil and fry for 4–4½ minutes on each side, depending on the thickness of the fish, until it is cooked through and richly golden brown. Lift onto some kitchen paper, leave to drain briefly, then transfer to serving plates. Toss the anchovy vinaigrette through the lettuce leaves and pile alongside the fish. Arrange the anchovy fillets to one side, sprinkle each piece of fish and the plate with a little *pimentón*, and serve.

Bacalao fritters with allioli

This recipe comes from my friend Aitor, one of the greatest young chefs that I know. I can't resist making these fritters every time I have a party, and serving them with plenty of *allioli* (garlic mayonnaise) on the side for dipping or just with some lemon juice. Enjoy them as soon as they are cooked, while they are puffed up, crisp and golden and piping hot.

Serves 8 (makes approx. 30 fritters)

250g *bacalao* (salt cod)

200g floury potatoes, cut into small chunks

sunflower or olive oil, for deep-frying

1 tablespoon extra virgin olive oil

1 garlic clove, crushed

30g plain flour

1 large free-range egg, beaten

2 tablespoons chopped flat-leaf parsley

fine sea salt and freshly ground black pepper

1 quantity Allioli (see page 227), or lemon wedges, to serve

Knock the excess salt off the cod and place it, skin-side up, in a bowl. Cover with plenty of cold water and leave to soak for 24 hours, changing the water every 6 hours or so. After this time, take a small piece of fish from the thickest part and taste it. If it doesn't taste too salty, it's ready to use, but remember: salt cod needs to be a little bit salty and also it will taste a slightly more salty once it is cooked.

Put the salt cod into a pan with 600ml cold water. Bring to the boil over a medium heat, turn off the heat and leave for 10 minutes. Lift the fish onto a plate with a fish slice and leave to cool. Add the potatoes to the water, bring back to the boil and simmer for 10 minutes until tender. Drain, reserving the cooking water, return them to the pan and mash until smooth. Flake the salt cod into a bowl, discarding the skin and any bones, and coarsely mash with the end of a rolling pin (or use a large pestle and mortar if you have one).

Heat the oil for deep-frying to 180°C (use a cooking thermometer). Meanwhile, warm the olive oil and garlic in a medium pan over a medium heat. As soon as the garlic is sizzling, add 150ml of the reserved cooking water and bring to the boil. Add the flour, reduce the heat to low and beat vigorously until the mixture is smooth and thickens slightly. Remove from the heat, leave to cool slightly, then gradually beat in the beaten egg to make a smooth paste. Stir in the mashed potatoes, salt cod, chopped parsley and a little salt and pepper to taste.

Drop 6–8 heaped teaspoons of the mixture, well-spaced apart, into the hot oil and cook for 4 minutes, turning them over halfway through, until they are crisp and golden. Drain each batch briefly on kitchen paper while you cook the rest. Serve hot with allioli or lemon wedges for squeezing.

Chicken in beer

The smell of this dish cooking reminds me of home, and my mother's cooking, but of course my mother being typically Spanish, never used mustard and butter in her recipe. She would always serve it with *patatas fritas* (see page 117) but it would also be good with Olive Oil Mash (see page 33).

Serves 4

1.5kg chicken, jointed into 8 pieces and skinned

1 teaspoon sweet *pimentón*

25g plain flour

3 tablespoons olive oil

25g butter

500g onions, halved and thinly sliced

6 whole cloves

1 teaspoon fennel seeds

1 tablespoon sugar

4 fresh bay leaves

2 teaspoons Dijon mustard

250–275ml lager-style beer

250ml chicken stock

2 teaspoons red wine vinegar

sea salt and freshly ground black pepper

Sprinkle the pieces of chicken all over with the *pimentón*, ½ teaspoon salt and some black pepper. Then coat in the flour and knock off the excess. Heat the olive oil in a flameproof casserole. Add the chicken pieces to the casserole and fry for about 4 minutes on each side until golden brown. Lift out onto a plate and set aside.

Melt the butter in the casserole, then add the onions, cloves, fennel seeds, 2 teaspoons of the sugar, the bay leaves and some salt and pepper. Cover and fry over a medium heat, stirring now and then, for 15 minutes until the onions are soft and nicely caramelised.

Uncover and stir in the remaining sugar and the mustard, then the beer, chicken stock and 1 teaspoon of the vinegar. Return the chicken pieces to the pan, bring to the boil, cover and simmer for 30 minutes until the sauce has thickened and the chicken is tender. Uncover and stir in the remaining vinegar and some salt and pepper to taste. Serve hot.

Carpaccio of veal with baby broad beans and lemon

The beef from this region is famous all over Spain. The value placed on dairy and beef cattle means herds are jealously guarded and meticulously cared for, grazing on lush pasture most of the year. The meat is sold according to age at slaughter: *ternera* (veal), at a maximum of 10 months old, is very popular and either sliced very thin and fried briefly or roasted; *anojo* is 10–18 months old; and *cebon*, 18–30 months old, is marbled with fat and full of flavour. I like to use veal rather than beef for carpaccio as the flavour is more delicate and the colour looks beautiful on the plate.

Serves 6

250g piece of veal loin

350g small podded broad beans

For the dressing

1 tablespoon lemon juice

1 teaspoon Dijon mustard

4 tablespoons extra virgin olive oil

2 teaspoons chopped mint

sea salt and freshly ground black pepper

To garnish

3–4 small mint leaves, finely shredded

small piece of Manchego cheese

Wrap the loin of veal tightly in clingfilm to form a cylindrical shape and freeze for 2 hours or until it becomes firm enough to slice.

Meanwhile, drop the broad beans into a pan of boiling salted water and cook for 3 minutes until just tender. Drain and refresh under cold water, then pop the bright green beans out of their skins into a bowl.

Make a slightly thick dressing by whisking the lemon juice and mustard together, then gradually whisking in the oil and some salt and pepper to taste.

Remove the veal from the freezer and, with the clingfilm still in place, cut it across into very thin slices. Remove the pieces of clingfilm and arrange the slices, slightly overlapping, over the base of 4 large plates.

Stir the chopped mint into the dressing. Stir 1 tablespoon of the dressing into the broad beans and adjust the seasoning if necessary. Drizzle the remaining dressing over the veal, then scatter the broad beans over the top. Sprinkle with the shredded mint, then use a sharp vegetable peeler to shave the Manchego cheese over each portion. Serve straight away.

Veal chops with black-eyed beans, pancetta and cabbage

Asadors **(simple restaurants where you can enjoy the local food and probably a glass of cider) are very popular in northern Spain.** *Chuleton* **(a large beef rib chop) is often used, but thick cut veal chops in my opinion are just as good. The beans and cabbage that accompany this dish celebrate some of the most highly revered ingredients from this region: dried beans and cabbage or** *grelos*. *Grelos* **are not available outside Spain, but cavolo nero or even curly kale are two very good alternatives.**

Serves 4

7 tablespoons extra virgin olive oil
1 medium onion, finely chopped
¾ teaspoon crushed dried chillies
300g black-eyed beans, soaked overnight in cold water
4 bay leaves
1 tablespoon fennel seeds
1 head of garlic, cloves separated, peeled and finely chopped
leaves from an 18cm rosemary sprig, finely chopped
4 x 500g veal chops, cut about 2.5cm thick
150g pancetta or smoked bacon lardons, cut into small dice
200g cavolo nero leaves or curly kale, torn into small pieces
150ml chicken stock
freshly grated nutmeg
sea salt and freshly ground black pepper

Heat 3 tablespoons of the olive oil in a medium pan, add the onion and ¼ teaspoon of the crushed dried chillies, cover and fry gently for 10 minutes until soft. Drain the beans and stir them into the pan with the bay leaves and 700ml cold water. Bring to the boil, part-cover and leave to cook over a gentle heat for 1¼–1½ hours, stirring now and then, until the beans are tender and the liquid has almost disappeared.

While the beans are cooking, lightly crush the fennel seeds (using a pestle and mortar if you have one), then mix in the remaining chilli flakes, half the chopped garlic, the rosemary, 2 tablespoons of the remaining olive oil, 1 teaspoon sea salt and some freshly ground black pepper. Rub this mixture over both sides of each veal chop and set aside in the fridge for 1 hour.

Heat a ridged or flat cast-iron griddle over a high heat. Lower the heat slightly, add the chops and cook for 6–8 minutes on each side until cooked through but still pink and juicy. The temperature at the centre of the meat should register 60°C on a meat thermometer. Remove from the griddle to a plate, cover loosely with foil and leave to rest for 5 minutes.

While the chops are cooking, finish off the beans. By the time they are tender, there should be very little liquid remaining – the beans should just be nicely moist. Remove and discard the bay leaves, stir in ½ teaspoon salt, cover and set aside.

Heat the remaining olive oil in a wide shallow pan, add the pancetta or lardons and fry for 2–3 minutes until lightly golden. Add the remaining garlic, fry for a few seconds, then stir in the cavolo nero or curly kale and stir-fry for 2 minutes until it begins to wilt. Add the chicken stock, cover and cook over a low heat for 8–10 minutes until tender. Stir in the cooked beans and season to taste with some nutmeg, salt and pepper. Serve with the veal chops.

Beef, red pepper and pimentón stew

I think the best beef comes from the north of Spain. The Spanish tend to eat beef much younger than people do in the UK and one of the most popular ways of preparing it is simply barbecued over a charcoal fire. Known as a *chilindron* in Spain, this is one of the most famous dishes from Navarra, the Basque Country and, further east, Aragon. A *chilindron* is more traditionally made with lamb, slow-cooked with plenty of dried and fresh red peppers from those regions, but I also love it made with beef. This recipe is just perfect for entertaining when you don't want to spend too much time in the kitchen. In Spain most stews are served with fried potatoes, but mash or rice would be excellent too.

Serves 6

3 dried choricero peppers
25g dried wild mushrooms, such as porcini
1.5kg blade or chuck steak
4–6 tablespoons extra virgin olive oil
100g diced pancetta, streaky bacon or Serrano ham
2 large onions, chopped
10 garlic cloves, thinly sliced
1 tablespoon sweet *pimentón*
1 tablespoon hot *pimentón*
300ml white wine,
400g skinned, chopped tomatoes, fresh or canned
1 tablespoon chopped rosemary
4 bay leaves
3 large red peppers
sea salt and freshly ground black pepper

Slit open the dried peppers and remove the stalks and seeds. Put them into a small bowl and cover with boiling water. Put the dried mushrooms into another small bowl and cover with 150ml hot water. Leave both to soak for 1 hour. Cut the beef into 3cm chunks and season well with salt and pepper.

Heat 2 tablespoons of the oil in a flameproof casserole over a medium-high heat. Lightly brown the beef in batches, transferring each batch to a bowl once it is done, and adding a little more oil when necessary.

Drain the mushrooms and peppers, reserving the mushroom soaking water. Squeeze out the excess liquid from the mushrooms and scrape the red pepper flesh away from the skins, discarding the skins. Add another 2 tablespoons of the oil to the casserole along with the pancetta, bacon or ham and, when it is lightly golden, add the onions. When they are beginning to colour, add the garlic and mushrooms and continue to cook until the onions are soft and lightly golden. Stir in both the sweet and hot *pimentón* and cook for a further 2 minutes.

Add the wine to the casserole and simmer until reduced by half. Return the beef and any juices to the casserole with the tomatoes, rosemary, bay leaves, choricero pepper flesh, ½ teaspoon salt and some black pepper. Add enough of the mushroom soaking water so that the liquid comes about two-thirds of the way up the beef and stir well. Cover and simmer gently for about 2½–3 hours, or until the beef is tender.

Meanwhile, grill the red peppers under a high heat, turning them now and then, until their skins are quite black. Drop them into a plastic bag and leave to cool, then break them open and remove the stalks and seeds. Peel off the skin and cut the flesh into thin strips. Stir into the stew 10 minutes before the end of the cooking time, together with a little more seasoning to taste. Serve the stew hot.

Beef chuleton with fried green peppers

When I was young I would regularly make myself a dish of potatoes and green peppers fried in olive oil, topped with a fried egg, especially mid-morning after a late night out. In the north of Spain *chuleton*, a large beef rib chop, is often served with fried *pimientos de Padrón*, those fiery little green peppers from Galicia, but these can be difficult to get hold of in the UK. Long thin Turkish green peppers work particularly well in this dish, or you can use ordinary green peppers: just cut them into quarters lengthways. And if you find Pardron peppers, use about 250g.

Serves 2–3

4 tablespoons olive oil, plus extra for the beef

8 long Turkish green peppers, deseeded and cut into 1cm-wide strips

3 fat garlic cloves, finely chopped

leaves from a 6cm rosemary sprig, finely chopped

1.5kg forerib of beef on the bone

sea salt and freshly ground black pepper

Preheat your barbecue to high or place a ridged cast-iron griddle over a high heat. Heat the oil in a large frying pan over a medium heat. Add the green peppers and fry for 12–15 minutes, turning regularly, until they are soft and nicely coloured. Add the garlic and rosemary and fry for a further 1–2 minutes. Season to taste with salt and pepper and set aside to keep warm.

Meanwhile, rub the forerib of beef with some oil and season well all over with salt and pepper. Barbecue or griddle the beef for about 6–7 minutes on each side for medium rare, or until the centre of the meat registers 65°C on a meat thermometer. Transfer it to a board, cover with foil and leave it to rest for 5 minutes, during which time the internal temperature will rise to 70°C.

To serve, cut the meat away from the bone and then diagonally, like a steak, into slices. Serve with the fried green peppers and some *patatas fritas* (see page 117).

Blue cheese with two apple compotes

I love salty, tangy blue cheese served with a sharp yet sweet apple compote and here I have given two variations. Allow about 50g of cheese per person and serve the compotes at room temperature. Choose a variety of apple that doesn't collapse during cooking. Cox and Braeburn both work well. Membrillo is a paste made from quinces, which is known as the perfect accompaniment to Manchego, but the addition of apple makes it amazing with blue cheese. One of my favourite blue cheeses from Spain is Cabrales from Asturias, which is really strong and pungent and always a winner on a cheeseboard.

Serves 4–6

For the zesty apple and lemon compote

4 large, firm dessert apples, peeled, cored, quartered and cut into large dice

finely grated zest of 1 large lemon and 3 tablespoons lemon juice

30g caster sugar

For the apple and membrillo compote

50g unsalted butter

4 large, firm dessert apples, peeled, cored, quartered and each quarter cut into 3 slices

50g membrillo, thinly sliced

1 tablespoon light muscovado sugar

1½–2 tablespoons lemon juice

¼ teaspoon ground cinnamon

2 tablespoons pressed apple juice

To serve

50g Picos Blue, La Peral or Cabrales cheese per person

For the zesty apple and lemon compote, mix the apples with the lemon zest and juice, and sugar, cover and leave to marinate for 30 minutes. Transfer the mixture to a saucepan, place over a medium heat, cover and leave to cook gently for 5 minutes until the apples are just tender. Uncover, increase the heat slightly and cook for a further 4–5 minutes, or until the excess liquid has evaporated. Remove and leave to cool.

For the apple and membrillo compote, melt the butter in a large, non-stick frying pan, add the apple slices in a single layer and fry gently for 4–5 minutes, turning over halfway through. Lift the slices onto a plate and pour off the excess butter. Add the membrillo to the pan with the sugar, lemon juice, cinnamon and apple juice and cook gently, stirring, until you have a smooth, jam-like sauce. Return the apple slices to the pan and stir to coat them in the sauce. Remove from the heat and leave to cool.

Baked cheesecakes with blueberries

The north of Spain is renowned for its prouduction of milk, which of course results in plenty of cheese and dairy desserts. We call cheesecakes *quesadillas*. This recipe is a big seller in Pizarro, where Maria, my pastry chef, changes the fruit according to the season – blueberries in summer, spiced quince in autumn and caramelised oranges in winter (see page 93).

Serves 6

450g full-fat cream cheese
125g caster sugar
1½ tablespoons cornflour
pinch of salt
2 medium free-range eggs
100ml soured cream
icing sugar, for dusting

For the blueberries

4½ tablespoons lemon juice
75g caster sugar
225g blueberries
1 teaspoon arrowroot

Tightly wrap some foil around the base of 6 poaching rings, 7cm wide and 6cm deep, then line the base and sides with greaseproof paper. Place on a baking tray.

Preheat the oven to 110°C/gas mark ¼. Put the cream cheese into a bowl and beat with an electric hand mixer until smooth and creamy. Beat in the sugar, cornflour, salt and eggs, then stir in the soured cream. Pour the mixture into the moulds and bake for 35–40 minutes until set but still slightly wobbly in the centre. The cheesecakes will continue to firm up as they cool. Remove from the oven and leave to cool. These can be chilled if you wish, but are best served at room temperature.

For the blueberries, put the lemon juice and sugar into a small pan and leave over a low heat until the sugar has dissolved. Add the blueberries, bring to a gentle simmer and cook for 1 minute. Mix the arrowroot with 1 teaspoon cold water, stir in to the fruit and cook for about 30 seconds until thickened. Transfer to a small bowl and allow to cool.

If you chilled the cheesecakes, remove them from the fridge 30 minutes or so before serving. Gently slide them out of their moulds and carefully peel off the lining paper from the bases. Put onto serving plates and then peel away the strip of paper from the sides. Dust the tops of the cheesecakes with icing sugar, spoon the blueberries around and serve.

Orange-scented apple buñuelos

Buñuelos **are crisp deep-fried fritters, popular all over Spain. I came up with the idea for these one day when I had a few apples to use up and needed a quick dessert to serve to friends, and I have to say they were very well received. I love to serve them with the Crema Catalana Ice Cream on page 60.**

Serves 6

For the batter

100ml whole milk

½ teaspoon caster sugar

100g plain flour

½ teaspoon fast-action dried yeast

pinch of salt

1 large egg, separated

3 tablespoons vintage cider

1 tablespoon olive oil

olive or sunflower oil, for deep-frying

For the orange-scented apples

3–4 small dessert apples, such as Cox

finely grated zest of ½ orange

1 tablespoon orange juice

1 tablespoon orange-flavoured liqueur, such as Grand Marnier

To finish

50g caster sugar

1 teaspoon ground cinnamon

For the batter, warm the milk with the caster sugar. Sift the flour, yeast and salt into a bowl. Make a well in the centre, add the egg yolk and gradually whisk in the milk and cider followed by the oil to make a smooth batter. Cover with clingfilm and set aside in a warm place for 1 hour until frothy.

Quarter, core and peel the apples and cut each piece into 3 wedges. Put them into a bowl with the orange zest, orange juice and orange liqueur and mix well together. Set aside for 1 hour alongside the batter.

When you are ready to cook the fritters, heat some oil for deep-frying to 180°C (use a cooking thermometer). Whisk the egg white in a clean bowl into soft peaks and gently fold into the batter.

Using a fork, lower one piece of apple at a time into the batter so that it takes on a thin, even coating, and then drop it into the hot oil. Cook, 6 pieces at a time, for 3 minutes, turning them over halfway through, until crisp and golden. Remove with a spoon and drain briefly on plenty of kitchen paper while you cook the remainder.

Mix the caster sugar with the ground cinnamon, sprinkle over the fritters and serve straight away while they are still hot and crisp.

Crema catalana ice cream

Crema catalana **is served all over Spain. Not unlike a crème brulée, though not cooked in the oven, it is an orange-flavoured thick custard, traditionally set in a shallow terracotta dish, topped with a thin layer of caramel just before serving. I decided one day to take things a step further by churning the custard in an ice-cream machine and folding some crushed caramel in at the end. It worked really well and makes a lovely accompaniment to the apple fritters on page 58.**

Makes 500ml

200ml whole milk
1 cinnamon stick
finely grated zest of 1 small lemon
finely grated zest of 1 small orange
4 large free-range egg yolks
100g caster sugar
300ml double cream

For the caramel

125g caster sugar
80ml cold water

Put the milk, cinnamon stick, lemon and orange zest into a saucepan and bring to the boil. Remove from the heat and set aside for at least 30 minutes to infuse.

Beat the egg yolks and sugar together in a bowl. Bring the milk back to the boil, gradually whisk into the egg-yolk mixture, then strain back into the cleaned-out pan. Cook over a gentle heat, stirring constantly, for 3–4 minutes until the mixture thickens and lightly coats the back of a wooden spoon. Remove from the heat, cool, then stir in the cream and refrigerate overnight.

To make the caramel, line a baking tray with greaseproof paper. Put the sugar and cold water into a small pan and leave over a low heat to dissolve. Then bring to the boil and cook until it turns into a brick-red caramel. Pour the mixture onto the baking sheet and tilt the tray back and forth to spread the mixture into a thin, even layer. Leave to get cold, then break into pieces using the handle of a knife.

Either churn the ice-cream mixture in an ice-cream machine or pour it into a shallow container and freeze until almost solid. Scrape into the bowl of a food processor and blend briefly until smooth, then return to the container and freeze once more. Repeat this 2–3 times more until the mixture is very smooth. If serving straight away, you can churn some of the caramel pieces into the ice cream. Otherwise, sprinkle over the top just before serving.

THE EAST

THE EAST: INTRODUCTION

Barcelona feels like a second home to me. When I arrive in this city, the first morning I go to the famous Boqueria food market to have breakfast – normally a slice of tortilla and some *pan con tomate*. Whether for work or pleasure, I love my trips to Barcelona and always leave with a great taste in my mouth. I find the entire Catalonia region to be very open-minded and cosmopolitan, yet it also manages to maintain its own language and traditions.

Catalonia is rich in gastronomic delights. Its perfect position between the Pyrenees and the Mediterranean provides a wealth of speciality ingredients. I love to cook with the wild mushrooms, shrimps from the port of Palamo, and capers with the olives and oils from the region. And let's not forget the cava, sparkling white or rosé wine, which I often use in my dishes, as well as serving when there is an excuse to celebrate.

The region of Murcia is another of Spain's 'market gardens', producing many of the country's vegetables, but in the northwest of Murcia, where four rivers cross a mountainous region, lies Calasparra, which has been growing rice since the 14th century. The quality of Calasparra rice is recognised by its Denominación de Origen status and it is one of my favourites. I use it for my rice dishes, including paella, which is from neighbouring Valencia.

Valencia is known throughout the world for paella, vibrantly coloured with saffron and *pimentón* and brimming with the best seasonal ingredients of the region and the sea, but there are many other Spanish rice dishes that you have to try. The black rice dish *arroz negro* and soupy rice dish *caldoso* on pages 77 and 82 are both spectacular. Valencia is also the home of my dear friend María José San Román. Everyone knows her as 'the queen of saffron' as she incorporates it so beautifully in her rice dishes. If ever you go to Alicante, you must visit one of her restaurants: Monastrell has a wonderful and ever-changing tasting menu while the Tavern of the Gourmet has a more relaxed atmosphere.

The dried fruits are of excellent quality in these eastern regions, a reminder of Spain's Moorish past that persists in the cuisine, and almonds and hazelnuts are grown for the production of the famous nougat (*turrón*) from Alicante – a sweet treat that is found on every table in Spain at Christmas time. Nuts, especially blanched almonds, are used in Spanish cuisine to flavour and thicken dishes such as stews and soups as well as sauces and desserts.

LLIMONAS
a Kilo€
1'70

MERCAT
St JOSEP
LA BOQUERIA

Wild mushroom, watercress and blue cheese tart

The hills and mountains of Spain provide the perfect growing conditions for wild mushrooms and nowhere do the Spanish love to go picking these delicacies more than in the north-eastern regions. There you will find chanterelles, pied bleu, pied de mouton, trompette de la mort, oysters, porcini and saffron milk cap. Wild mushrooms go extremely well with blue cheese and walnuts, so this is my recipe for a tart using all three. I always make this for my friend Catriona when she comes over to help me with my website.

Serves 8

300g mixed wild mushrooms
2 tablespoons olive oil
40g watercress leaves
100g Picos Blue cheese, crumbled
300ml double cream
4 large free-range eggs
sea salt and freshly ground black pepper

For the pastry

50g walnut pieces
225g plain flour, plus extra for dusting
65g chilled butter, cut into pieces
65g chilled lard, cut into pieces

Preheat the oven to 200°C/gas mark 6. For the pastry, spread the walnuts on a baking tray and roast for 7–8 minutes. Remove and leave to cool. Tip them into a food processor and add 50g of the flour. Grind together briefly until the nuts are finely chopped. Add the remaining flour and ½ teaspoon salt, together with the butter and lard, and process briefly once more until the mixture resembles fine breadcrumbs. Tip the mixture into a bowl and stir in 2 tablespoons cold water until the mixture comes together into a ball, then turn out onto a lightly floured surface and knead briefly until smooth. Roll out thinly on a little more flour and use to line a lightly greased loose-based 23cm flan tin with sides 4cm deep. Chill for 20 minutes.

Put a baking tray on the middle shelf of the oven and leave it to get hot. Line the pastry case with foil and a thin layer of baking beans, slide it onto the baking sheet and bake for 20 minutes. Remove the foil and beans and return to the oven for 5 minutes until the pastry is lightly golden. Remove and set aside while you make the filling. Lower the oven temperature to 190°C/gas mark 5.

Clean the wild mushrooms thoroughly by brushing away any dirt with a dry pastry brush and wiping them with a damp cloth if necessary. Heat 1 tablespoon of the olive oil in a large frying pan over a high heat, add half the mushrooms and some seasoning and fry briskly for 1 minute until they have softened slightly and any excess moisture has evaporated. Tip onto a plate and repeat with the remainder.

Scatter the mushrooms, watercress leaves and blue cheese evenly over the base of the pastry case. Beat together the cream and eggs with some seasoning, pour the mixture into the tart and return it to the baking sheet. Bake for 30–35 minutes until set and lightly golden. Serve warm, cut into wedges.

Wild mushroom and Manchego cheese canalóns

Take care to clean the wild mushrooms properly by using a pastry brush and wipe them with a slightly damp cloth, only if you really have to, but never ever wash them. Mushrooms are like sponges and absorb water very easily, which will ruin them when you come to cook them. If you are using ready-made pasta for this dish, ensure you find a brand that is rolled out quite thinly. *Canalóns* are a national dish of Barcelona, introduced by Italian restaurateurs in the 19th century and so they closely resemble Italian cannelloni. My mother always makes *canalóns* with minced meat and tomato sauce, but I have to say that my recipe is better than hers!

Serves 8

25g dried wild mushrooms, such as porcini

1 tablespoon olive oil

40g butter, plus extra for greasing

100g shallots, finely chopped

3 garlic cloves, finely chopped

500g mixed wild mushrooms, cleaned
    and sliced

leaves from 3 large thyme sprigs

25g plain flour

300ml whole milk

freshly grated nutmeg

16 *canaló* wrappers or 8 large sheets
    fresh lasagne pasta, cut into
    12 x 15cm rectangles

75g Manchego cheese, finely grated

sea salt and freshly ground black pepper

For the béchamel sauce

1.2 litres whole milk

75g butter

65g plain flour

Put the dried mushrooms into a small bowl and cover with boiling water. Leave to soak for 30 minutes, then drain well, squeezing out all the excess water, and slice thinly. Bring a large pan of well-salted water to the boil.

Heat the oil and butter in a large frying pan. Add the shallots and garlic and cook gently for 5 minutes until soft but not brown. Add the soaked and fresh wild mushrooms and the thyme, increase the heat to high and stir-fry for 4–5 minutes or until all the excess moisture has evaporated and the mushrooms are tender.

Stir the flour into the pan, then gradually stir in the milk. Bring to the boil, stirring, and leave to simmer for 5 minutes, stirring now and then. Season to taste with nutmeg, salt and pepper. Allow to cool slightly.

Meanwhile, drop the *canaló* wrappers or lasagne sheets into the pan of hot water, turn off the heat and leave to soak for 5 minutes until just tender. Drain, run under cold water and then quickly separate and lay side by side on some clingfilm. Spoon a generous 2 tablespoons of the mushroom mixture along one short edge of each wrapper, roll up and set aside on the clingfilm.

Preheat the oven to 200°C/gas mark 6. For the béchamel sauce, bring the milk to the boil in a pan. Melt the butter in another pan, stir in the flour and cook over a low heat for 3–4 minutes, stirring, without letting it brown. Gradually stir in the hot milk and bring to the boil, stirring. Leave to simmer for 5 minutes, stirring frequently, until smooth and thick and then season to taste with salt and pepper.

Pour about one quarter of the sauce into a lightly buttered shallow baking dish just big enough to hold the *canalóns* in a single layer and spread it over the base. Arrange the *canalóns* on top. Pour over the remaining sauce so that they are evenly covered and sprinkle with the grated cheese. Bake for 25–30 minutes until richly golden brown and bubbling.

Bacalao, potato and salad onion tortilla

The most popular tortilla in Spain is one made with just potatoes. However, this one, flavoured with *bacalao* (salt cod) and salad onions, is pretty hard to beat. The trick to making a good tortilla is to add the cooked ingredients to the bowl of beaten eggs, not the other way around, to stir the mixture a little as soon as it is put into the pan until it just begins to thicken, then to cook it slowly until set almost all the way through. Flipping it over takes a bit of practice, but by using a large plate or pan lid you will soon get the hang of it. Don't be scared of making a tortilla. It is one of the easiest things in the world to master if you follow these few simple rules.

Serves 6

300g piece *bacalao* (salt cod)
450g potatoes
6 tablespoons extra virgin olive oil
120g continental salad onions, trimmed and thinly sliced
8 large free-range eggs
2–3 tablespoons chopped flat-leaf parsley
sea salt and freshly ground black pepper

Knock the excess salt off the *bacalao* and place it, skin-side up, in a bowl. Cover with plenty of cold water and leave to soak for 24 hours, changing the water every 6 hours or so. After this time, take a small piece of fish from the thickest part and taste it. If it doesn't taste too salty, it's ready to use, but remember: salt cod needs to be a little bit salty and also it will taste slightly more salty once it is cooked. Drain the pieces of salt cod and put them into a pan with enough cold water to cover. Bring to the boil, remove from the heat, cover and set aside for 10 minutes to cook gently in the heat of the water. Then lift out onto a plate and, when it is cool enough to handle, break the fish into flakes, discarding the skin and any bones. Cover and set aside.

Cut the potatoes into 1cm-thick chunky matchsticks. Heat 4 tablespoons of the olive oil in a 23cm non-stick frying pan, add the potatoes and cook, stirring now and then, for 15 minutes or until just tender but not browned. You are not aiming for chips here. Lift onto a plate with a slotted spoon, add the salad onions to the pan and cook for 2–3 minutes until just soft. Remove from the heat and leave to cool slightly.

Beat the eggs in a mixing bowl with ½ teaspoon salt and some pepper. Stir in the fried potatoes, salad onions, flaked *bacalao* and chopped parsley. Wipe the frying pan clean. Reheat the pan with another tablespoon of the olive oil over a medium heat and, when it is hot, pour in the tortilla mixture and cook, stirring it gently with a wooden spoon, for about 1 minute until thickened slightly. Smooth the mixture down, neaten up the edges and leave to cook over a gentle heat for 10 minutes or until golden brown underneath and almost completely set.

Cover the pan with an upturned plate or large pan lid, turn them over together so that the tortilla is now on the lid and return the pan to the heat, adding the remaining oil. Slide the tortilla back into the pan and cook for a further 2–3 minutes until just cooked through. Remove from the pan and leave to cool slightly. Serve warm, cut into wedges.

Olive oil mash with poached eggs and truffle butter

The Spanish love eggs, but before I moved to England I rarely had the opportunity to eat poached eggs because in Spain we usually serve them fried or boiled, scrambled or set in tortillas. Poached eggs have become one of my favourite ways of eating them and nothing is more pleasing than cutting into a perfectly soft yolk. People have queried the combination of poached eggs and mash because of the softness of both textures, but, I promise you, it works!

Serves 4

1 teaspoon white wine vinegar

4 very fresh large, free-range eggs

For the olive oil mash

900g floury potatoes, such as Maris Piper

4 garlic cloves, peeled but left whole

1 bay leaf

4 tablespoons extra virgin olive oil

120ml whole milk

For the truffle butter

50g butter

1 x 10g black truffle

1 teaspoon truffle oil

sea salt and freshly ground black pepper

Cut the potatoes into large chunks. Put them into a pan of well-salted water with the garlic cloves and bay leaf. Bring to the boil and simmer for 15–20 minutes or until the potatoes are tender. Meanwhile, bring 1.2 litres water to the boil in a small pan. Drain the potatoes well, removing and discarding the garlic cloves and bay leaf, then press them through a potato ricer back into the pan. Beat in the olive oil, salt to taste and enough of the milk to make a smooth, creamy mash. Cover, return it to a low heat and keep warm.

Lower the heat under the small pan of water so that the water is barely simmering, and add a large pinch of salt and the vinegar. Swirl it vigorously to ceate a whirlpool and crack in one of the eggs. Leave it to poach for 3 minutes, then lift out with a slotted spoon onto a plate. Repeat with the rest of the eggs. Keep the water simmering.

For the truffle butter, melt the butter in a small pan. Peel the black scaly outer layer from the truffle and very finely grate it into the butter. Stir in the truffle oil and some salt and pepper to taste. Keep hot.

Return the poached eggs to the simmering water and leave to heat through for 30 seconds, then lift out and drain briefly on kitchen paper.

Spoon some of the hot olive oil mash into 4 small warmed bowls and place a poached egg on top. Spoon some of the truffle butter over each egg, sprinkle with a little sea salt and serve.

Fresh and smoked salmon tartare

I must be mad to use Spanish smoked salmon when the British Isles – Scotland in particular – produce some of the best smoked salmon in the world, but I love that made by my friend Carlos Piernas, who is well-known in Spain for the mild smoky flavour of his salmon. He is situated in the most beautiful national park in Catalonia where I spent an amazing week shooting photographs for this book. He marinates his salmon with sugar and salt and then smokes it very lightly. When I go to see him I spend one lunch eating all the different cuts of salmon, from the less fatty tail to the most incredible *taro* (the piece below the belly). This is not his recipe, but I dedicate it to him for his hospitality. The salmon is left a little more raw and moist than other versions.

Serves 4

400g salmon fillet, skinned

100g smoked salmon

2 tablespoons capers, rinsed, drained and finely chopped

50g shallots, very finely chopped

2 tablespoons chopped flat-leaf parsley

6 cornichons, finely chopped

8–10 dashes Tabasco sauce, according to taste

1 teaspoon sea salt flakes

2 tablespoons extra virgin olive oil

2 teaspoons lemon juice

4 medium free-range egg yolks

freshly ground white pepper

fingers of toast, to serve

Thinly slice the salmon fillet and smoked salmon, then cut them into long thin strips about 5mm wide. Put them into a bowl with the capers, shallots, parsley, cornichons, Tabasco, sea salt, olive oil, lemon juice and white pepper. Mix together well, spoon into the centre of 4 chilled plates and shape into a neat pile. Make a small dip in the top of the mixture and add an egg yolk to each one. Serve with the fingers of toast.

Gambas à la gabardina with lemon

I can't tell you where to find the best *gambas à la gabardina* because there are so many delicious recipes from all over Spain, but I think the best one I ever tried was in Paramos. The prawns cook inside the batter, keeping their succulence, so that when you bite into them you have a wonderful rich, sweet flavour.

Serves 4

450g (approx. 20) large raw unshelled prawns

olive oil or sunflower oil, for deep-frying

2 large free-range egg whites

fine sea salt

lemon wedges, to serve

For the batter

110g plain flour

¼ teaspoon hot *pimentón*

5 tablespoons olive oil

75ml lager-style beer

75ml cold water

Make the batter 30 minutes before you want to start cooking. Sift the flour, *pimentón*, and a good pinch of salt into a mixing bowl. Make a well in the centre, add the oil, lager and water and beat well together until you have a smooth batter. Cover and leave it to stand for 30 minutes.

Meanwhile, peel the prawns, leaving the last tail segment in place. Shortly before cooking, heat some oil for deep-frying to 190°C (use a cooking thermometer). Whisk the egg whites in a bowl into soft peaks and gently fold into the batter.

Holding each prawn by its tail, dip it into the batter and add it to the hot oil. Cook 5–6 at a time for 2½–3 minutes until crisp and golden. Drain briefly on kitchen paper while you cook the remainder and serve hot with the lemon wedges.

Pan-fried sea bream with a salad of oranges, red onion, capers and black olives

The region of Valencia is famous for its citrus groves and particularly its oranges. There they regularly make a salad using flaked salt cod, oranges, onion and black olives, but I often like to substitute the salt cod with a freshly cooked fillet of fish; the fresh, summery flavours go so well together. This salad is also lovely made with blood oranges when they are in season.

Serves 4

8 x 75g sea bream fillets

1 tablespoon olive oil

sea salt and freshly ground black pepper

For the salad

4 small oranges

1 small red onion

4 teaspoons small capers, rinsed and drained

16 good-quality black olives, pitted and halved

For the vinaigrette

1 tablespoon freshly squeezed orange juice

1 tablespoon sherry vinegar

1½ tablespoons extra virgin olive oil

4 teaspoons chopped flat-leaf parsley

For the salad, cut a thin slice off the top and bottom of each orange and slice away all the skin, ensuring the white pith is completely removed. Then cut either side of each segment of fruit, close to the dividing membrane, down into the centre of the orange, and drop the segments into a bowl.

Halve the onion and very thinly slice it, on a mandolin if possible, then separate the slices. Add them to the bowl of orange segments with the capers and black olives and mix together gently.

For the vinaigrette, whisk the orange juice, sherry vinegar and olive oil together in a small bowl and add some seasoning to taste. Stir in the chopped parsley.

Heat a large non-stick frying pan over a medium heat. Rub the bream fillets with oil and season on both sides. Add the fillets, skin-side down, to the pan and cook for 4–5 minutes until the skin is crisp and golden. Carefully turn the fillets over with a palette knife and cook for a further 2 minutes, then remove the pan from the heat and leave the fish to finish cooking in the heat of the pan.

Gently stir 4 teaspoons of the vinaigrette into the salad and adjust the seasoning to taste. Spoon some of the salad onto each plate and rest the fish fillets on top. Drizzle a little more of the vinaigrette over the fish.

Rice with prawns, pancetta, tomato and peas

This simple rice dish, flavoured with prawns and pancetta, can be cooked in a shallow flameproof casserole, a terracotta _cazuela_, or large frying pan rather than a traditional paella pan, and makes an ideal supper dish for feeding a crowd.

Serves 6

½ teaspoon saffron (about 20 threads)
1 litre chicken stock
5 tablespoons extra virgin olive oil
200g smoked pancetta, cut into short fat strips, or smoked bacon lardons
1 medium onion, finely chopped
4 garlic cloves, thinly sliced
350g skinned, chopped tomatoes, fresh or canned
1 teaspoon sweet _pimentón_
400g paella rice (Calasparra or Bomba)
350g fresh or frozen peas
18–20 large, raw unpeeled prawns
sea salt and freshly ground black pepper

Shake the saffron strands around in a slightly hot frying pan for a few seconds until dry but not coloured, then tip into a small mortar or coffee cup and grind to a powder with a pestle or a wooden spoon. Add a splash of the chicken stock and set aside.

Heat 3 tablespoons of the olive oil in a 28–30cm terracotta _cazuela_ or shallow flameproof casserole. Add the pancetta and fry until it is crisp and golden, then stir in the onion and garlic and fry gently for 8–10 minutes until soft and lightly golden. Stir in the tomatoes and _pimentón_ and fry for a further 2–3 minutes until the tomatoes start to soften. Stir in the saffron mixture, the rest of the stock and 1½ teaspoons salt and bring to the boil. Sprinkle in the rice, stir once and leave to simmer a little vigorously for 6 minutes. Sprinkle over the peas, then lower the heat and leave to simmer more gently for 14 minutes until the rice is _al punto_, or still with a little bite to it.

Shortly before the rice is cooked, rub the prawns with the remaining oil and season well with salt and pepper. Heat a large frying pan/flat cast-iron griddle over a high heat. Place the prawns side by side in the pan, lower the heat to medium, and cook for 2–2½ minutes on each side until just cooked through (they will continue to cook once they are on top of the rice). Arrange the prawns on top of the rice, turn off the heat, cover the casserole with a tea towel or pan lid and leave to rest for 5 minutes before serving.

Sautéed squid with black rice and allioli

It's not always easy to find uncleaned squid and preparing it yourself does involve a bit of work. The alternative is to buy ready-prepared squid from a fishmonger, together with a sachet or two of squid ink, which will guarantee that you end up with enough ink to give the rice its characteristic black colour.

Serves 6

750g uncleaned squid (or buy ready-prepared with 1–2 sachets of squid ink)
1 litre fish stock
7 tablespoons extra virgin olive oil
2 medium onions, finely chopped
2 large garlic cloves, finely chopped
200g skinned, chopped tomatoes, fresh or canned
150ml dry white wine
400g paella rice (Calasparra or Bomba)
sea salt and freshly ground black pepper
1 quantity Allioli (see page 227), to serve

If you are using uncleaned squid you need to remove and save the ink sacs from inside the pouches. Pull the heads away from the pouches, taking with them the intestines and clear quill. Locate the ink sacs (they resemble pearly blue-white sacs), detach them and set them aside. Cut the tentacles away from the heads, just in front of the eyes and discard the rest. Pull the fins away from the bodies and pull away the grey membranous skin from both. Rinse out the squid pouches with cold water, then slice them and the fins across into 5mm-wide strips. Separate the tentacles into pairs. To extract the ink from the sacs put some of the fish stock into a bowl and, one at a time, slit open the sacs and rinse them out in the stock. Discard the sacs.

Heat 3 tablespoons of the oil in a 46cm paella pan. Add the onions and garlic and fry gently for 6–8 minutes until soft and lightly golden. Add the tomatoes and cook for 4–5 minutes until softened, then stir in the wine and simmer for a further 3–4 minutes until it has almost disappeared. Stir in the inky fish stock and remaining stock and bring to the boil. Scatter over the rice, stir once so that it is evenly distributed around the pan and leave to simmer quite vigorously for 6 minutes. Lower the heat and leave to simmer gently for a further 14 minutes until all the stock has been absorbed and the rice is pitted with small holes. Turn off the heat, cover with a clean tea towel or a large pan lid and leave to rest for 5 minutes.

Meanwhile, heat another 2 tablespoons of oil in a large frying pan. Add half the squid and stir-fry over a high heat for 2 minutes, seasoning it as it cooks, until nicely browned and just cooked through. Tip on to a plate and repeat with the remainder. Uncover the rice, scatter over the squid and serve with the allioli.

Pasta with chorizo and mussels

Pasta is popular in the east of Spain. You might wonder why a Spanish chef is cooking with pasta, but so many Italian chefs are cooking wonderful dishes with chorizo, so why not? I created this dish with my friend Diego in Barcelona. I still remember buying the mussels from La Boqueria, the famous food market in that city, and marrying the flavours with a very nice glass of red wine from Priorat.

Serves 4

6 tablespoons extra virgin olive oil

3 garlic cloves, finely chopped

½ teaspoon crushed dried chillies

400g skinned, chopped tomatoes, fresh or canned

1kg fresh mussels

400g dried spaghetti

6 tablespoons dry white wine

200g cooking chorizo sausage, skinned and diced

2 tablespoons chopped flat-leaf parsley

sea salt and freshly ground black pepper

Put 4 tablespoons of the olive oil, the garlic and chillies in a large frying pan or saucepan and place it over a medium-high heat. As soon as the garlic is sizzling, add the tomatoes and simmer gently for 15 minutes until well reduced, quite thick and just starting to stick to the bottom of the pan.

Meanwhile, bring a large pan of well-salted water to the boil. Wash the mussels, pull out the beards from between the tightly closed shells and discard any that are open and won't close when tapped on a work surface. Add the spaghetti to the boiling water and cook for 10–11 minutes or until *al punto* – still with a little bite.

Heat another large pan over a high heat, add the mussels and the wine, cover and cook for 2–3 minutes, shaking the pan now and then, until all the mussels are only just open. Take care not to overcook them at this stage. Tip them into a colander placed over a bowl to collect the cooking juices. Stir all but the last tablespoon or two of the cooking liquid into the tomato sauce and continue to simmer until the sauce has reduced and thickened once more, but is a little more moist than before. Season to taste with salt and pepper. Remove half of the larger mussels from their shells.

Heat the remaining olive oil in a frying pan, add the chorizo and fry gently for 1 minute until lightly golden. Drain the spaghetti, return to the pan and add the tomato sauce, cooked mussels, chorizo sausage and chopped parsley. Toss well together and serve.

Grilled sausages with arrocina beans, garlic and sage

For this dish it is really important to get meaty continental-style fresh sausages. Those from Spain called *butifarra blanca*, or from southern France such as Toulouse, or Italy's *salsicche*, are 100 per cent pure meat, flavoured with spices, without the filler which is so often present in British-style sausages. The arrocina beans are small, sweet and meaty dried beans. If you can't get hold of them, use dried haricot or cannellini beans.

Serves 4

300g dried small white beans, such as arrocina, soaked overnight in cold water
1 medium onion, halved
4 cloves
4 bay leaves
1 head of garlic, halved, plus 3 garlic cloves, finely chopped
4–8 large fresh meaty pork sausages (*butifarra* if possible)
4 tablespoons extra virgin olive oil
12 large sage leaves, finely chopped
350g vine-ripened tomatoes
sea salt and freshly ground black pepper

Drain the beans, put them into a pan with 1 litre cold water and bring them to the boil. Meanwhile, stud the onion halves with the cloves. Skim the scum from the surface of the beans, add the onion halves, bay leaves and garlic bulb, lower the heat, cover and leave to simmer gently for 1–1½ hours or until the beans are tender, adding 1 teaspoon salt 5 minutes before the end of cooking. Drain, remove and discard the onion, bay leaves and garlic, and set aside.

Heat a ridged or flat cast-iron griddle or a heavy-based frying pan over a high heat. Rub the sausages with a little of the oil, add them to the griddle or pan, lower the heat to medium and cook for 8–10 minutes, turning them now and then, until they are golden brown and cooked through.

Meanwhile, skin the tomatoes, quarter them and scoop the seeds into a sieve set over a bowl. Rub through the juices with a wooden spoon, and cut the flesh into small pieces.

Shortly before the sausages are ready, heat the remaining olive oil and the chopped garlic in a large frying pan over a medium heat. As soon as the garlic is sizzling, add the sage and leave it to cook for a few seconds. Add the beans and stir gently for 3–4 minutes until they have heated through. Stir in the tomatoes and their juices and cook gently for a further 2–3 minutes, so that the pieces of tomato retain their shape. Season generously to taste (beans need plenty of seasoning) with salt and pepper and serve with the grilled sausages.

Caldoso with quail, wild mushrooms, artichokes and black olives

Spain has many great rice dishes, paella being the most famous. *Caldoso*, a soupy rice dish, follows the same cooking principles but just uses double the amount of stock, so it is more like a rice casserole than a paella. This is a surprisingly easy dish to make, and extremely comforting and tasty to eat. Do try it for a change the next time you think about making a paella. If quail are a bit tricky to find, use skinned chicken thighs instead – it will still taste delicious.

Serves 4

25g dried wild mushrooms, such as porcini

4 oven-ready quail

2 tablespoons extra virgin olive oil

1 cooking chorizo sausage (approx. 100g), skinned and cut into small dice

1 medium onion, chopped

2 large garlic cloves, finely chopped

350g small ceps, sliced, or button chestnut mushrooms, halved if large

leaves from 2 large thyme sprigs

leaves from a 16cm rosemary sprig, chopped

½ teaspoon sweet *pimentón*

250g vine-ripened tomatoes, skinned and chopped

1.2 litres chicken stock

300g paella rice (preferably Calasparra)

4 bay leaves

280g jar artichoke hearts or bases in olive oil, drained and halved if large

50g good-quality black olives, pitted

sea salt and freshly ground black pepper

2 tablespoons chopped flat-leaf parsley, to garnish

Put the dried mushrooms into a small bowl and cover with boiling water. Leave to soak for 30 minutes. Meanwhile, cut along either side of the backbone of each quail with kitchen scissors, remove it and discard. Open out each quail flat and cut in half along the breastbone, then into quarters by cutting the legs away from the breasts. Remove the small rib bones from the underside of each breast and season all the pieces well with salt and pepper.

Heat the oil in a large flameproof casserole or pan. Add half the quail pieces skin-side down and fry for 3–4 minutes until golden brown. Turn over and fry for 2 minutes more, then remove from the pan onto a plate. Repeat with the remaining quail pieces.

Add the chorizo to the casserole and fry for 1 minute until lightly golden. Add the onion and garlic and fry for 5–6 minutes over a medium heat until soft and lightly golden. Drain the rehydrated mushrooms and squeeze them dry. Add them to the onions and garlic with the fresh mushrooms, thyme, rosemary and a little more seasoning and fry, stirring, for another 4 minutes. Stir in the *pimentón*, fry for 30 seconds, then add the tomatoes and cook for 2 minutes until softened.

Return the quail pieces to the pan with the stock and bring to the boil. Stir in the rice and bay leaves and season to taste with salt and pepper. Lower the heat and leave to simmer for 18 minutes, stirring now and then, until the rice is almost cooked.

When the rice is nearly done, stir in the artichokes and black olives and simmer for 2 minutes, stirring. Serve in large warmed soup plates, scattered with the chopped parsley.

Roast chicken with cava and apples

In Spain, roast chicken is not traditionally served with a slightly thickened gravy as in the UK, but after living here for 10 years or more I like to do some things the British way. However, I take a tip from my mother and combine chicken with apples, which doesn't seem to be very British. Why not? It's delicious, especially if you serve it with some more cava!

Serves 4–6

1 x 1.5kg free-range chicken
4 bay leaves
2 large thyme sprigs
olive oil, for greasing the bird
2 medium onions, cut into thin wedges
6 garlic cloves, thinly sliced
1 x 750ml bottle cava
4 small dessert apples, such as Cox
25g butter
2 teaspoons caster sugar
¼ teaspoon ground cinnamon
100ml chicken stock
1 teaspoon soft butter
1 teaspoon plain flour
sea salt and freshly ground black pepper

Preheat the oven to 200°C/gas mark 6. Season the cavity of the chicken with salt and pepper and then stuff with the bay leaves and thyme. Tie the legs together with string, then rub all over with olive oil and season well with salt and pepper. Place in the centre of a large roasting tin and roast for 30 minutes.

Remove the roasting tin from the oven and scatter the onions and garlic around the chicken. Stir them into the cooking juices, season lightly, pour 50ml of the cava over the bird and return it to the oven for 45 minutes, basting it every 10 minutes with a another 50ml of the cava.

While the chicken is roasting, quarter, core and peel the apples and cut into small wedges. Melt the butter in a frying pan, add the apples and fry them for 2 minutes until they begin to brown. Turn the slices over, sprinkle with the sugar and cinnamon and continue to fry for a further 2 minutes until they are just tender and nicely golden. Remove from the heat.

When the chicken is cooked and the juices run clear, lift it onto a board, wrap it in foil and leave it to rest for 10 minutes. Scoop the onions out of the roasting juices, add them to the apples and mix well together. Season lightly to taste and keep warm over a low heat.

Tip the roasting tin so that the remaining pan juices pool at one end and skim off the excess fat. Then place the tin over a medium-high heat, add another 100ml of the cava and the stock and scrape the base of the tin with a wooden spoon to release all the caramelised juices. Strain into a small pan and simmer for about 10 minutes until reduced and well-flavoured. Mix the soft butter with the plain flour, whisk it into the gravy and simmer gently for 2–3 minutes. Season to taste with salt and pepper.

Carve the chicken. Spoon some the onions and apples onto each warmed plate and put the chicken on top. Pour over the gravy and serve.

Braised chicken with tomatoes, salsify and almonds

There was a time when the only chickens you could buy in Spain were those that were truly free-range with very little meat covering the breast and dark, almost gamey-tasting meat. Today Spanish chicken are more similar to the birds reared in the UK and braised chicken is second only to *pollo al ajillo* **(chicken fried with garlic) in popularity. If you can't get salsify, use young slender parsnips, cut lengthways into quarters – the dish will taste just as good.**

Serves 6

1kg salsify
juice of 1 lemon
6 tablespoons extra virgin olive oil
4 garlic cloves, peeled
30g blanched almonds, toasted
5g flat-leaf parsley, plus extra, chopped, to garnish
500ml chicken stock
1 x 1.75kg chicken, jointed into 8–10 pieces
100g pancetta or streaky bacon lardons
1 large onion, finely chopped
400g skinned, chopped tomatoes, fresh or canned
1 teaspoon caster sugar
40g plain flour
sea salt and freshly ground black pepper

Peel the salsify and cut each piece lengthways into three, dropping them immediately into a bowl of cold water, acidulated with the lemon juice, to prevent them from turning brown. Bring a large pan of well-salted water to the boil. Add the salsify and simmer for 15–20 minutes or until just tender. Drain well, then leave to dry on a clean tea towel or kitchen paper.

Heat 2 tablespoons of the olive oil in a shallow flameproof casserole or large deep frying pan. Add the garlic cloves and fry them gently for 2–3 minutes until soft and golden brown. Put them into a mini food processor with the toasted almonds, parsley leaves and 3–4 tablespoons of the stock. Blend to a smooth paste, then set aside.

Add another 2 tablespoons of the olive oil to the pan and place over a medium-high heat. Add half of the chicken pieces, season them with salt and pepper and fry for about 8–10 minutes until a deep golden brown all over. Lift onto a plate and repeat with the rest of the chicken.

Add the pancetta or bacon to the pan and fry until crisp and golden. Lift out with a slotted spoon and set aside with the chicken. Add the onion to the pan and fry gently for 8–10 minutes until golden brown. Add the tomatoes and sugar, reduce the heat slightly and simmer for 5 minutes until the tomatoes have broken down and thickened into a sauce.

Meanwhile, heat the remaining oil in another non-stick frying pan over a medium-high heat. Working in batches, season the salsify, then dust in the flour and fry, turning occasionally, until crisp and golden brown all over. Transfer each batch to a tray lined with kitchen paper.

Stir the remaining stock into the tomato sauce, add the fried chicken and pancetta or lardons, cover and simmer for 20 minutes. Stir in the salsify and simmer, uncovered, for a further 15 minutes until the chicken is tender and the sauce has reduced and thickened. Stir in the almond and garlic paste and some seasoning to taste and simmer for a further 5 minutes. Serve garnished with chopped parsley.

Duck with orange, Spanish style

I love the classic combination of duck with oranges, but this dish is a little different with the addition of cinnamon and honey. The total cooking time I allow for a roast duck is 15 minutes per 450g, which results in a very slightly pink and juicy meat. I use Valencian oranges because they are the best, obviously!

Serves 4

1 x 2kg oven-ready duck

fine sea salt and freshly ground black pepper

watercress, to garnish

For the orange sauce

4–5 oranges

25g caster sugar

4 tablespoons sherry vinegar

450ml chicken or duck stock

2 teaspoons honey

1 x 5cm cinnamon stick

1 tablespoon lemon juice

1 teaspoon arrowroot

If you have time, unwrap the duck, dry it well inside and out with kitchen paper and leave it somewhere cool for the skin to dry off, overnight if possible.

Preheat the oven to 230°C/gas mark 8. Season the cavity of the duck with salt and pepper, and the skin just with salt. Place it on a rack in a large roasting tin and roast for 20 minutes. Then remove it from the oven and pour the excess fat from the tin into a small bowl. Lower the oven temperature to 180°C/gas mark 4, return the duck and continue to roast for 40 minutes, pouring the fat from the tin into a small bowl every 15–20 minutes. (Don't discard it: duck fat is excellent for roast potatoes.)

Meanwhile, for the sauce, peel the zest from half of 1 orange and cut it into long, fine shreds. Drop them into a pan of boiling water, leave for 5 seconds, then drain and refresh under cold water. Set aside to drain on kitchen paper. Next, cut a thin slice off the top and bottom of 2 of the oranges and slice away all the skin, ensuring the white pith is completely removed. Then cut either side of each segment of fruit, close to the dividing membrane, down into the centre of the orange, and drop the segments into a bowl. Set aside. Squeeze the juice from the remaining oranges and measure out 150ml of juice.

Put the sugar and vinegar into a small pan and leave over a low heat until the sugar has dissolved. Increase the heat and boil rapidly until it has turned into a dark amber-coloured caramel. Remove from the heat and carefully add the stock (take care as it will splutter quite a bit), the honey, orange juice and cinnamon stick. Bring to the boil and simmer rapidly until reduced by three-quarters to 150ml. Remove the cinnamon stick, stir in the lemon juice and a little seasoning to taste and bring back to a simmer. Mix the arrowroot with 1 tablespoon water, stir into the sauce and simmer for 1 minute, until thickened and clear. Stir in the shredded orange zest and keep warm.

Remove the duck from the oven, lift it onto a board, cover loosely with foil and leave to rest for 5–10 minutes. Add the orange segments to the sauce and bring it back to a simmer. Carve the legs off the duck and cut each one in half at the joint. Cut each of the breasts away from the carcass in one piece and cut each one lengthways into long thin slices. Arrange the meat on warmed plates, spoon over the sauce and serve, garnished with the watercress.

Cava and lemon sorbet with candied lemon peel

There is nothing better than to finish a meal with a cleansing sorbet. In Spain, people often use a lemon sorbet between courses to cleanse the palate. I never understand that as I think the best way to clean the palate is a nice glass of wine! This sorbet is best served soon after churning and freezing, and doesn't improve on keeping. The candied lemon peel adds that necessary sweetness.

Serves 10–12

4 large juicy lemons

350g caster sugar

75g liquid glucose, plus 1 tablespoon

pinch of salt

1 x 750ml bottle of cava

For the candied lemon peel, pare wide strips of peel from the lemons using a sharp vegetable peeler, ensuring none of the bitter white pith is included. Cut the parings lengthways into 3mm-wide strips. Put them into a pan with enough cold water to cover, bring to the boil and simmer for 15 minutes, then drain and refresh under cold water.

Put 200g of the sugar, 1 tablespoon of the liquid glucose, a pinch of salt and 500ml water into a clean pan. Bring to the boil, add the blanched lemon peel, and leave to simmer until the mixtures registers 110°C on a sugar thermometer. Remove from the heat, lift the strands of peel out of the syrup with a fork and curl them attractively on a large baking tray lined with greaseproof paper. Leave to go cold, then finely chop 50g of it and set aside. Reserve some of the prettiest strands for decoration and store the remainder in an airtight container for a future batch of sorbet.

For the sorbet, pour half the cava into a pan and add the remaining sugar and liquid glucose. Bring slowly to the boil, stirring to dissolve the sugar, then remove from the heat and leave to cool. Meanwhile, squeeze the pared lemons to yield about 200ml of juice. Stir the remaining cava into the cooled syrup with the lemon juice, strain the mixture into a bowl, cover and leave to chill overnight.

The next day, churn the sorbet mixture in an ice-cream machine. Alternatively pour it into a shallow container and freeze until almost solid. Scrape into the bowl of a food processor and blend briefly until smooth, then return to the container and freeze once more. Repeat this 2–3 times more until the mixture is very smooth. Stir in the chopped candied lemon peel towards the end of churning or after blending for the final time spoon back into the container and freeze for at least 6 hours or until firm. Serve in scoops, decorated with the reserved pieces of candied peel.

Roasted hazelnut ice cream

Reus, in the province of Tarragona, is the centre of hazelnut production in Spain, but today the industry is seriously threatened by competition from Turkey. In an effort to help the Spanish industry and halt the trend for using cheaper imported hazelnuts, the EU awarded the nuts from this region a mark of quality called the Denominación de Origen. Today they are highly revered and go into the production of many sweets and nut pastries of the region. This is one of my favourite ice creams.

Serves 6–8

For the hazelnut paste

225g shelled hazelnuts

1 large egg white

50g icing sugar, sifted

2 tablespoons hazelnut liqueur (optional)

For the ice cream

1 vanilla pod

200ml whole milk

3 large egg yolks

100g caster sugar

300ml double cream

For the hazelnut paste, preheat the oven to 200°C/gas mark 6. Spread the nuts on a baking tray and roast for 12–15 minutes or until richly golden. Remove and leave to cool, then rub off the skins in a clean tea towel. Drop half the nuts into a food processor and grind very finely. Tip into a bowl and grind the remaining nuts. Return the first batch to the food processor with the egg white, sugar and hazelnut liqueur, if using, and blend to a smooth paste.

For the ice cream, slit open the vanilla pod and scrape out all the seeds. Put the pod and seeds into a pan with the milk and slowly bring to the boil. Gently whisk the egg yolks and sugar together in a bowl until pale and creamy. Remove the vanilla pod from the milk and gradually whisk the hot milk into the egg yolks. Return the mixture to a clean pan and cook over a low heat, stirring, until the mixture lightly coats the back of a wooden spoon. Leave to cool, then strain into the food processor and blend with the hazelnut paste. Transfer to a bowl, cover and chill overnight.

The next day, stir the cream into the hazelnut custard, add the remaining ground nuts and churn the ice-cream mixture in an ice-cream machine. Alternatively, pour it into a shallow container and freeze until almost solid. Scrape into the bowl of a food processor and blend briefly until smooth, then return to the container and freeze once more. Repeat this 2–3 times more until the mixture is very smooth, then return to the freezer for 6 hours or until firm and ready to use.

Apricots in cava

This is a really simple and quick dessert. It celebrates the very best of summer fruits – just make sure your apricots are ripe and sweet.

Serves 6–8

12 ripe apricots

3 tablespoons caster sugar, or to taste

4 tablespoons peach liqueur

200g raspberries

500ml chilled cava or sparkling rosé wine

Peel the apricots, then halve the fruit, remove the stones, and slice the fruit into a glass serving bowl. Sprinkle over the sugar and peach liqueur and toss together gently. Cover and chill until needed.

Shortly before serving, sprinkle the raspberries over a plate and lightly crush them with the back of a fork. Stir them into the apricots, pour over the sparkling wine and serve straight away.

Blood orange sorbet

I love blood oranges so much I wait eagerly for them to come back into season. This sorbet is simple to make and one of the nicest ways in which to enjoy their sweet sharp flavour and beautiful deep red colour.

Serves 6–8

100g caster sugar

40g liquid glucose

120ml water

12 blood oranges

juice of 1 lemon

Put the sugar, liquid glucose and water into a pan and bring slowly to the boil, stirring occasionally to dissolve the sugar. Remove from the heat and leave to cool.

Squeeze the blood oranges to yield about 600ml of juice. Stir it into the cooled syrup with the lemon juice, strain into a bowl and chill overnight.

The next day, churn the sorbet mixture in an ice-cream machine. Alternatively pour it into a shallow container and freeze until almost solid. Scrape into the bowl of a food processor and blend briefly until smooth, then return to the container and freeze once more. Repeat this 2–3 times more until the mixture is very smooth. Spoon back into the container and freeze for at least 6 hours or until firm. This is lovely served in scoops with a mixture of orange and blood orange wedges, dressed with a little sugar and lemon juice.

Almond bizcocho with caramel oranges

A *bizcocho* is a simple loaf-shaped cake, which is regularly served for afternoon tea in Spain. My sister Isabel always makes one when I visit her. I love to eat *bizcocho* whilst it is still slightly warm from the oven. However, it also makes an excellent dessert, especially if served with caramel oranges so that the delicious juices soak into the sponge. A scoop of ice cream on the side is pretty good too. If you can't get blood oranges – sadly they are around only for a few short weeks during the winter months – use small juicy normal oranges instead.

Serves 8

200ml olive oil, plus extra for greasing

175g plain flour

2 teaspoons baking powder

pinch of salt

100g ground almonds

175g caster sugar

3 large, free-range eggs, lightly beaten

finely grated zest of 1 orange

100ml freshly squeezed orange juice

For the caramel oranges

8 blood oranges or small, juicy oranges

200g caster sugar

6 tablespoons freshly squeezed orange juice, strained

For the caramel oranges, cut a slice off the top and bottom of each orange, then slice away all the skin, ensuring the white pith is completely removed. Cut each orange across the segments into slices, reserving all the juices. Put the sugar into a large pan with 120ml cold water. Leave over a low heat until the sugar has dissolved, then bring to the boil and boil rapidly until the syrup has turned into a brick-red caramel. Remove from the heat and plunge the base of the pan into cold water, to stop it cooking any further. Stand back (as it will splutter slightly) and add the orange juice. The caramel will form a lump in the bottom of the pan. Return it to a low heat and stir until it dissolves again. Leave to cool very slightly, then, while it is still liquid, pour over the sliced oranges and chill for at least 1 hour.

For the almond *bizcocho*, preheat the oven to 170°C/gas mark 3. Grease a 1kg loaf tin with olive oil and line with greaseproof paper. Sift the flour, baking powder and salt into a mixing bowl and stir in the ground almonds and caster sugar. Make a well in the centre and add the beaten eggs, olive oil, orange zest and juice. Gradually mix the dry ingredients into the wet to make a smooth batter.

Pour the mixture into the prepared tin and bake for about 1 hour, covering the surface loosely with a sheet of paper after about 50 minutes, once it is a rich golden brown. A skewer, pushed into the centre of the cake, should come away clean. Remove the cake from the tin and peel back the lining paper. Leave to cool on a wire rack.

To serve, cut the cake into 16 slices. Place a slice onto each plate and spoon some of the caramel oranges partly over the slice. Top with another slice and drizzle over a little more caramel syrup.

Chocolate and hazelnut tart

This is one of the best tarts I have ever eaten and is a must for all chocolate and nut lovers. Once I start to eat it, I cannot stop. Try to serve it shortly after it comes out of the oven – still slightly puffed up and warm – but you can serve it cold if you like, and even a few days later. Serve warm with cream or ice cream, or cold with a cup of coffee.

Serves 10–12

For the filling

275g shelled hazelnuts

125g good-quality dark chocolate
  (at least 70% cocoa solids)

90g soft butter

150g caster sugar

finely grated zest of 1 orange

2 medium free-range eggs

1 tablespoon plain flour

3 tablespoons sweet sherry, such as Oloroso

For the pastry

225g plain flour, plus extra for dusting

pinch of salt

65g icing sugar

125g chilled butter, cut into small pieces

1 large egg yolk

5 teaspoons sweet sherry, such as Oloroso

For the pastry, sift the flour, salt and icing sugar into a food processor. Add the butter and process briefly until the mixture resembles fine breadcrumbs. Mix the egg yolk with the sherry. Tip the crumbed mixture into a bowl, stir in the egg yolk and sherry mixture and bring the dough together into a ball. Turn out onto a lightly floured surface and knead briefly until smooth. Shape into a flat disc, wrap in clingfilm and chill for 15 minutes.

Remove the pastry from the fridge and roll it out thinly on a lightly floured surface. Use to line a 25cm, loose-based tart tin with sides 4cm deep. Refrigerate again for 20 minutes.

Put a baking sheet on the middle shelf of the oven and preheat it to 200°C/gas mark 6. Line the pastry case with foil and a thin layer of baking beans and bake for 15 minutes. Remove the foil and beans and bake for another 4–5 minutes until crisp and golden brown. Remove and set aside. Spread the hazelnuts onto a tray and roast for about 8 minutes until richly golden. Remove and allow to cool. Reduce the oven temperature to 170°C/gas mark 3.

For the filling, grind the hazelnuts finely in a food processor until they resemble coarse breadcrumbs, but leave some of them a little chunky. Break the chocolate into a small heatproof bowl set over a pan of barely simmering water. Take the pan off the heat and leave until the chocolate has melted, then lift the bowl off the pan and allow the chocolate to cool. Beat the butter, sugar and orange zest together in a bowl until light and fluffy. Beat in the eggs, one at a time, adding a little of the flour with the second egg to stop the mixture from curdling. Fold in the remaining flour, the ground hazelnuts, melted chocolate and lastly the sherry. Spoon the mixture into the pastry case and bake for 30 minutes, by which time it should be slightly risen and feel firm to the touch in the centre. Remove and leave to cool slightly before serving, and dust with icing sugar, if desired.

THE CENTRE

THE CENTRE: INTRODUCTION

Central Spain is the home of the conquistadors and Don Quixote, and includes my beloved Extremadura, which is where my family are from. My favourite time to visit is during autumn, when the saffron is being picked, peppers are being smoked to make *pimentón* and hunting becomes a national pastime.

Madrid is where I learnt about *nueva cocina*, working for my dear friend and mentor Julio Reoyo, whose restaurant is Mesón de Doña Filo. In the 16th century, people from all over Spain flocked to Madrid so, not only is it a melting pot, but it boasts many restaurants that specialise in dishes from every region. Should you be wondering why this chapter contains recipes using sea fish even though the area is landlocked, believe it or not, Madrid has the best fish market in Spain. And no visit to the capital should exclude a trip to the San Miguel market for tapas, or to one of the bars that surround it for a nice cold beer and a sandwich filled with deep-fried calamari… heaven on earth and the best cure for a hangover!

Extremadura used to be a bit off the beaten track for tourists, but its popularity is growing and, obviously being my home, I can see why! There are so many places in the region that you must see. Guadelupe is the town where Christopher Columbus came (first to gain sponsorship from King Ferdinand and Queen Isabella and the blessing of a safe voyage from the Virgin Mary of Guadalupe and second, on his successful return from the New World, to show thanks), carrying with him highly significant ingredients that we now automatically associate with Spain – peppers, tomatoes and potatoes. These were grown by the monks of Guadalupe, and they were the first to make *pimentón* by smoking and grinding the peppers into a powder. *Pimentón* gives chorizo its distinctive colour and intense flavour. Restaurants and bars in the city of Trujilo serve the local dish of *mijas* – breadcrumbs fried with olive oil and garlic and served with chorizo, fried peppers and *panceta*. Extremadura also produces *jamón Ibérico*, one of the finest of Spain's air-cured hams, and indeed all the products from the Ibérico pig – pork loin, morcilla, chorizo and the fresh meat. If you come to my bar or restaurant in London, you must try some of the different cuts of Ibérico, like *pluma*, the fillet, and the cheeks.

The arid, high plateau of Castile-La Mancha is particularly famous because of the fictional knight Don Quixote, but in culinary terms it is the source of Manchego cheese, and, in my opinion, the best saffron in the world. The game from this area is exceptional – I particularly love the partridge. As in all of Spain, it is the simple, traditional fare eaten by the locals for centuries that marry the regional ingredients so perfectly. A rustic dish of beans, partridge and local herbs can be one of the tastiest meals you will ever have.

Further north, Castile and León is the heart of pulse-growing in Spain, in particular *garbanzos* (chickpeas), Pardina lentils and the *Judías* (white beans), which are used in regional everyday dishes. *Morcilla de Burgos*, a type of black pudding containing rice, is a gourmet delight. My favourite way of serving this morcilla is pan-fried, topped with a fried egg.

Aragón is a land of hard winters and very warm summers. I have included Aragón in this chapter because its key ingredients and style of cooking are similar to the rural areas in the centre. Lamb and game from the Pyrenees are integral to the local cusine, but to me, the most important of all products from this region is the *jamón de Teruel*, which has great aroma and flavour. The differences between this and the equally top-quality *jamón Ibérico* are the breed of pig, the feed and the curing process, so don't ever think these hams are the same!

If you are visiting any of these central regions, you must try the lamb. There is almost nothing better than a slow-roasted shoulder with some white wine, olive oil, thyme and garlic.

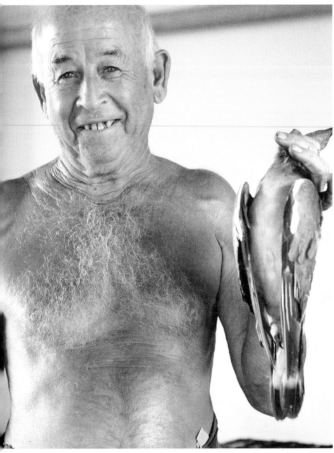

Chickpea soup with seared prawns, chorizo and pimentón oil

Chickpeas and chorizo are a common combination in Spain, but making a soup with these flavours is unusual. My tip is to add some prawns to give a little sweetness. Altogether, it is a very satisfying, winter warming dish.

Serves 4

8 tablespoons extra virgin olive oil

2 medium onions, chopped

½ teaspoon crushed dried chillies

300g dried chickpeas, soaked for
  24–48 hours in cold water

1 bay leaf

2 fat garlic cloves, thinly sliced

¾ teaspoon sweet *pimentón*

1 teaspoon freshly ground coriander seeds

juice of ½ lemon

12 large raw peeled prawns

1 x 100g cooking chorizo sausage, skinned
  and thinly sliced

sea salt and freshly ground black pepper

Heat 6 tablespoons of the oil in a large saucepan. Add the onions and crushed dried chillies, cover and fry gently for 10 minutes until the onions are very soft and lightly golden. Scoop half the onions into another pan and set aside. Drain the chickpeas and add them to the first pan with the bay leaf and 1 litre cold water. Bring to the boil, cover and simmer gently for 2–2½ hours or until the chickpeas are very tender. Remove and discard the bay leaf.

Shortly before the chickpeas are ready, place the second pan of fried onions over a medium heat. As soon as they are sizzling, stir in the garlic, ½ teaspoon of the *pimentón* and the ground coriander and fry gently for 2–3 minutes. Stir in the chickpeas and their cooking liquor and leave to cool slightly. Then blend, in batches if necessary, until very smooth. Return to the pan and stir in about 250ml more water, or enough to give the soup a good consistency. Stir in the lemon juice, season to taste with salt and pepper, and bring back to a gentle simmer over a low heat.

Heat the remaining oil in a frying pan over a medium heat. Add the prawns and sliced chorizo sausage and fry for 2 minutes until the prawns are just cooked through. Ladle the soup into warmed bowls and garnish with the fried prawns and chorizo. Add the remaining *pimentón* to the frying pan and leave to sizzle gently for a few seconds. Drizzle the oil over the soup and serve.

Melon, cherry tomato, cucumber and mint salad with Serrano ham

I think the saltiness of the ham and the sweetness of the melon work beautifully together. I love to add some crisp cucumber and ripe tomatoes to the melon as well, with finely shredded mint. Serve with crusty bread for an ideal summertime lunch or starter. This combination of ingredients is popular in all Mediterranean countries – but of course I use serrano ham and Spanish tomatoes. And you can make the ham crispy by frying it in some olive oil to give more texture to the dish.

Divide the melon into four; scoop out and discard the seeds. Slice the flesh away from the skin and cut it into small pieces, about the same size as the halved cherry tomatoes. Peel the cucumber, quarter it lengthways and cut into similar-sized pieces. Put the melon, tomatoes and cucumber in a serving bowl with the shredded mint and toss together gently until the mint is well distributed.

Make the vinaigrette by whisking the vinegar, honey and oil together with some salt and black pepper to taste. Stir into the salad. Arrange the Serrano ham slices on 4 plates and serve with the salad and fresh bread.

Serves 4

½ charentais or canteloupe melon

½ cucumber

175g vine-ripened cherry tomatoes, halved

1 tablespoon finely shredded mint

12 thin slices Serrano ham

For the vinaigrette

2 teaspoons red wine vinegar

½ teaspoon clear honey

1½ tablespoons extra virgin olive oil

sea salt and freshly ground black pepper

Braised peas and jamón with eggs

This dish was one of my favourites when I was a student. It is really easy to make and filling – perfect for your pocket. These braised peas (without the egg) would make a lovely side dish, maybe with a piece of simply grilled chicken or fish. You can bake this recipe in individual small dishes as well – easy for a simple supper for one after work. Add some chopped mint if you have some, to give freshness to the dish.

Serves 2

2 extra-large, free-range eggs

sea salt and freshly ground black pepper

For the braised peas

3 tablespoons olive oil

100g shallots, finely chopped

4 garlic cloves, thinly sliced

450g shelled peas, fresh or frozen

100ml homemade chicken stock

75g thinly sliced Serrano ham, finely shredded

Heat the olive oil in a medium frying pan. Add the shallots and garlic, cover and cook gently for 5 minutes until soft but not browned. Stir in the peas and chicken stock, part-cover and simmer gently for 5 minutes until the peas are tender and the liquid has reduced to leave them just moist. Stir in the Serrano ham, and season to taste with salt and pepper.

Break the eggs, spaced well apart, on top of the peas, season lightly and cover the pan with a well-fitting lid. Leave to cook gently for 5 minutes, or until the eggs are set to your liking. Eat with some crusty fresh bread.

Pardina lentils with soft goat's cheese and sherry vinegar

Pardina lentils, from Castile and León, are brown lentils that don't lose their skin or their bite. Use Puy lentils as an alternative.

Serves 4

350g pardina lentils

6 garlic cloves, 3 finely chopped and 3 left whole

3 bay leaves

6 tablespoons extra virgin olive oil, plus extra to serve

2 medium red onions, finely chopped

1½ teaspoons caster sugar

125g sun-dried tomatoes in oil, drained and chopped

12 spring onions, thinly sliced

3 tablespoons chopped flat-leaf parsley

2 tablespoons sweet Pedro Ximenez or balsamic sherry vinegar, plus extra to serve

150–200g soft rindless goat's cheese, sliced

sea salt and freshly ground black pepper

Put the lentils, the 3 whole garlic cloves and the bay leaves into a pan and cover with 5cm cold water. Bring to the boil and simmer for 20 minutes. Add 1 teaspoon salt and continue to cook for another 10 minutes until the lentils are just tender but still a little *al punto* – with a little bite. Drain, reserving the cooking liquid. Remove and discard the garlic cloves and bay leaves.

Heat half the olive oil in a deep frying pan, add the onions and sugar and fry gently for 5–6 minutes until soft. Add the chopped garlic and fry for a further 1–2 minutes. Stir in the warm cooked lentils and 150ml of the cooking liquid, the sun-dried tomatoes, spring onions, parsley, reserved vinegar and salt and pepper to taste. Bring back to a gentle simmer.

Spoon the lentils into shallow bowls and crumble the goat's cheese slices on top. Drizzle over a little olive oil and vinegar and serve.

Garlic prawn salad with Ibérico ham

Ibérico ham from Extremadura, in my biased opinion, is the best ham in the world. When I have a slice of it, I am transported to a spiritual place!

Serves 4

100g prepared curly endive

1 tablespoon extra virgin olive oil

20 large raw peeled prawns

2 garlic cloves, finely chopped

pinch of crushed dried chillies

1 red chilli, deseeded and finely chopped

8 thin slices of Ibérico ham

sea salt and freshly ground black pepper

For the vinaigrette

3 tablespoons extra virgin olive oil

1 tablespoon Pedro Ximenez sherry vinegar

½ teaspoon caster sugar

For the vinaigrette, whisk the olive oil with the vinegar, sugar and some salt and pepper to taste. Put the curly endive into a large bowl.

Heat a large frying pan over a medium-high heat. Add the olive oil and the prawns and season with some salt and pepper. Fry them for 1½ minutes on each side until just cooked through, adding the garlic and dried and fresh chillies to the pan as you turn them over.

Pour the vinaigrette over the curly endive and toss well together. Adjust the seasoning if necessary and divide between 4 plates. Arrange the prawns and ham slices alongside, and serve.

'Poor man's potatoes' with onions, peppers, garlic and thyme

This is traditionally fried in a large pan, but I find it easier to make in a large roasting tin. It is a great side dish with any roasted or barbecued meat. And, for a quick supper, it is wonderful topped with a couple of fried eggs. When I make this recipe I always wonder where the name came from – I think it is because the ingredients are so cheap and easily available and the dish is filling and tasty.

Serves 4

1kg waxy potatoes, such as Desirée
2 large red peppers
2 large green peppers
3 large red onions, cut into thin wedges
6 fat garlic cloves, thinly sliced
6 bay leaves
leaves from 4 large thyme sprigs
6 tablespoons olive oil
sea salt and freshly ground black pepper

Preheat the oven to 230°C/gas mark 8 and bring a large pan of well-salted water to the boil. Cut the potatoes across into 7–8mm-thick slices, drop them into the water, bring back to the boil and cook for 1–2 minutes until just tender when pierced with the tip of a knife. Drain well.

Halve the red and green peppers and remove and discard the stalks and seeds. Cut them into 1cm-wide strips. Put them into a large roasting tin (measuring about 30 x 40cm) with the potatoes, onions, garlic, bay leaves and thyme leaves. Season with 2 teaspoons sea salt and plenty of black pepper, pour over 4 tablespoons of the olive oil and toss well together. Spread everything out in a single even layer and drizzle over the rest of the olive oil.

Roast on the top shelf of the oven for 20 minutes, then remove the tin and turn the vegetables over. Return to the oven and roast for a further 20 minutes, until the potatoes are golden and the other vegetables are tender and nicely caramelised here and there. Serve straight away.

Seafood, potato and leek stew with saffron

Potatoes and saffron are a heavenly combination and this rich, warming stew is a favourite of mine. The best saffron in the world grows in La Mancha and is used in many many dishes in the centre of Spain. They call it 'oro rojo' – red gold. It is different from other saffrons because it is toasted on a very low heat over a fire. It adds warmth, colour and depth to a dish, but be careful not to use too much of it as the subtlety will be lost.

Serves 4

16 large raw unpeeled prawns

4 tablespoons olive oil

3 bay leaves

6 black peppercorns

400g piece of white fish fillet, such as haddock
   or cod

1 medium onion, chopped

2–3 garlic cloves, finely chopped

1 green pepper, deseeded and chopped

300g leeks, thickly sliced

½ teaspoon saffron strands

500g floury potatoes, cut into
   1.5cm pieces

2 tablespoons chopped flat-leaf parsley

sea salt

Peel the prawns, reserving the heads and shells. Heat 2 teaspoons of the oil in a medium pan, add the prawn heads and shells and sauté them for 2–3 minutes. Add 800ml water, the bay leaves, peppercorns and ½ teaspoon of salt and leave to simmer for 15 minutes. Strain and return to the pan. Add the fish, cover and simmer for 8 minutes until just cooked through. Lift the fish onto a plate and strain the stock into a large jug. You should be left with about 600ml. Flake the fish, discarding the skin and any bones and set aside with the stock.

Heat the remaining olive oil in a clean pan, add the onion and garlic, cover and fry gently until soft but not browned. Add the green pepper and leeks, cover again and fry gently for a further 3–4 minutes. Stir in the saffron, potatoes, prawn stock and another ½ teaspoon salt, bring to a simmer, cover once more and cook gently for 15 minutes until the potatoes are tender.

Crush some of the potatoes into the stew to thicken it a little, then stir in the prawns and flaked fish. Simmer for 2 minutes until the prawns are cooked through. Adjust the seasoning to taste, stir in the parsley and serve.

Pimentón-dusted monkfish on a warm potato, tomato and basil salad

The sweet paprika (*pimentón dulce*) is not normally used to marinate fish, but I use it for monkfish because of its meaty flavour. *Pimentón de la Vera* is made very close to my home town in Extremadura and is an ingredient I simply couldn't live without. The tomato and basil salad adds a refreshing lightness to the dish.

Serves 4

4 x 175g pieces of thick monkfish fillet

½ teaspoon sweet *pimentón*

2 tablespoons olive oil

sea salt and freshly ground black pepper

basil sprigs, to garnish

For the warm potato salad

600g waxy new potatoes

6 tablespoons extra virgin olive oil

2 tablespoons red wine vinegar

2 tablespoons wholegrain mustard

200g vine-ripened tomatoes, skinned, deseeded and diced

6 spring onions, thinly sliced

4 green queen olives, pitted and cut lengthways into thin strips

small handful of basil leaves, finely shredded

Preheat the oven to 200°C/gas mark 6. Season the monkfish with salt and set aside for 15 minutes.

Put the potatoes into a pan of cold salted water, bring to the boil and cook for 10–12 minutes or until tender. Meanwhile, pat the monkfish dry on kitchen paper and then sprinkle each piece generously all over with the *pimentón*. Heat the olive oil in an ovenproof frying pan, add the monkfish pieces and leave them to fry for 1½ minutes. Turn the pieces over, transfer the frying pan to the oven and roast for 10–12 minutes.

Returning to the potato salad, put the olive oil, vinegar and mustard into a large shallow pan and warm through over a low heat. Drain the potatoes and, as soon as you can handle them, quickly cut them into 2cm pieces. Add them to the warm dressing with the tomatoes, spring onions and olives and turn over gently until everything is coated with the dressing and heated through.

Remove the monkfish from the oven and carve each piece across into thick slices. Stir the shredded basil into the potato salad with some seasoning to taste and spoon it onto 4 warmed plates. Place the monkfish alongside, garnish with the basil sprigs and serve.

Roasted monkfish with Serrano ham, black olives and thyme

Monkfish can carry other strong flavours easily, and this combination is stunning. I always use *negra cacereña* olives as they are from my region, and together with the thyme they remind me of my lovely Extremadura. If you can't find *negra cacereña*, use proper, ripe black olives. They should have a lovely oiliness, not a dry, metallic flavour.

Serves 4

40g good-quality pitted black olives, finely chopped

1½ teaspoons finely chopped thyme leaves

2 anchovy fillets in olive oil, drained and finely chopped

1 garlic clove, finely chopped

4 x 175g pieces of thick monkfish fillet

8 thin slices of Serrano ham

2 tablespoons olive oil, plus extra to serve

sea salt and coarsely ground black pepper

watercress sprigs, to garnish

Preheat the oven to 200°C/gas mark 6. Mix together the black olives, thyme, anchovies and garlic. Cut a pocket lengthways into each piece of monkfish, taking care not to cut all the way through, and push an equal amount of the black olive mixture into each one. Pat the monkfish dry, season lightly with salt and pepper and then wrap each piece in 2 slices of the ham, securing the parcel at each end with string.

Heat the olive oil in an ovenproof frying pan. Add the ham-wrapped monkfish parcels and cook for 1½ minutes. Turn the parcels over, transfer the pan to the oven and roast for 10–12 minutes until cooked through.

Remove the monkfish from the oven and put onto a board. Remove the string. Cut each piece diagonally in half and arrange on 4 warmed plates. Drizzle a little oil around the outside of each plate, sprinkle with sea salt and some black pepper and serve garnished with the watercress.

Pan-fried John Dory with caramelised chicory, crisp-fried ham and mint

Where I grew up, we only ever used olive oil for cooking, which is why not many of my recipes are made with butter, but, for this dish, using butter with the olive oil to cook the chicory takes away its bitterness to achieve a wonderful caramelised flavour.

Serves 4

6 small heads of chicory
25g butter
4 tablespoons olive oil
4 teaspoons caster sugar
1 tablespoon lemon juice
8 thin slices of Serrano ham
4 x 200g thick, unskinned John Dory fillets, halved
4 large mint leaves, finely shredded
sea salt and freshly ground black pepper

Remove a layer of outer leaves from each head of chicory if they are damaged and trim the base if brown, but take care not to cut off too much or the leaves will separate. Cut each head in half lengthways through the base.

Heat the butter and 2 tablespoons of the oil in a large non-stick frying pan, add the chicory pieces and fry them for 3 minutes on each side until golden brown. Sprinkle over half the sugar, turn over and cook for a further 2 minutes. Sprinkle over the rest of the sugar, turn over once more and cook for a further 2 minutes. Sprinkle over the lemon juice and some seasoning to taste and fry for a final 2 minutes until the chicory is tender and nicely caramelised.

While the chicory is cooking, heat the remaining oil in another frying pan. Add 4 slices of the ham and fry them for 1 minute on each side until nicely golden. Lift onto a tray lined with kitchen paper and repeat with the remaining ham.

Season the pieces of John Dory, add them to the frying pan, skin-side down, and fry in the ham-flavoured oil for 2½–3 minutes on each side, pressing down on the pieces with a fish slice as they cook so that each side browns evenly.

Place 3 pieces of chicory into the centre of each plate and sprinkle them with the mint. Place the fillets of John Dory on top. Tuck 2 slices of crisp ham under each piece of fish, spoon some of the caramelised chicory juices around the edge of the plate and serve.

Pork chops with roasted vinegar onions

The quality of the meat is so important for pork chops, and that you cook them so they are juicy and succulent, not tired and dry. As everyone knows, I think Ibérico pork is the best, but, wherever you are, try to find local, free-range pork to get that superior flavour. Ibérico pork is now found on menus in good restaurants across the world – I even saw it on a menu in Hong Kong earlier this year – and thank you Peter for taking me there.

Serves 4

4 large pork chops on the bone, ideally Ibérico, cut 2.5cm thick
2 large garlic cloves
1 teaspoon sweet *pimentón*
3 tablespoons olive oil
2 tablespoons dry white wine
sea salt and freshly ground black pepper
1 quantity Olive Oil Mash (see page 33), to serve

For the vinegar onions

1kg red onions
3 tablespoons olive oil
3 tablespoons sherry vinegar
1 tablespoon caster sugar
1 tablespoon clear honey

Trim the rind from each pork chop, leaving behind the fatty edge if you wish, then lightly score the meat on both sides into a diamond pattern. Flatten the garlic cloves on a board, sprinkle with ½ teaspoon salt and crush into a smooth paste with the blade of a large knife. Mix with the *pimentón*, olive oil, white wine and a little more sea salt and some black pepper. Rub this mixture over both sides of each chop (but try not to get any on the fatty edge) and set aside, in the fridge, for at least 1 hour, or overnight.

Preheat the oven to 220°C/gas mark 7. Cut the red onions into quarters through the root end and then cut each piece into thin wedges. Put them into a large roasting tin with the olive oil, sherry vinegar, sugar and some salt and pepper and toss well together. Roast for 45–50 minutes, removing from the oven and turning them over every 10–15 minutes, until they are soft and nicely caramelised.

About 15 minutes before the onions are ready, heat a large flat griddle or heavy-based frying pan over a high heat until smoking hot. Lower the heat to medium, and, using tongs, hold the chops with their fatty edges on the hot griddle and cook for a couple of minutes until crisp and golden brown. Then lay them flat and sear for 1–2 minutes on each side until nicely browned. Transfer them to a roasting tin in which they will fit side by side and roast for 8 minutes or until cooked through, but still juicy in the centre. Remove from the oven, cover with foil and leave them to rest for 5 minutes.

Remove the onions from the oven and stir in the honey and a little more seasoning to taste. Serve with the pork chops and olive oil mash.

Patatas fritas, fried eggs and ham

My friend Bea Blaquez makes the best *huevos fritos rotos* in the world. Her secret is to use the very best ham and always the very best olive oil in which to fry the potatoes. This is the ideal dish to have late in the evening with a glass of good red wine.

Serves 2

450g Maris Piper potatoes
600ml extra virgin olive oil
4 large free-range eggs
75g slice of Ibérico or Serrano ham, cut into small dice
sea salt and freshly ground black pepper

Cut the potatoes lengthways into 5mm-thick slices, then cut the slices lengthways into thin chips. Pour the oil into a large deep frying pan and heat to 180°C (use a cooking thermometer). Add the chips, stir well and leave them to fry for 7–8 minutes until they are tender and golden brown.

Shortly before the chips are ready, spoon 2 large spoonfuls of the hot oil into another frying pan. Heat the oil until it just starts to smoke, then crack in the eggs, keeping them as far apart as you can, and fry them until the whites are set and the edges nice and crispy.

Lift the chips out of the oil and drain briefly on plenty of kitchen paper. Season with salt and pepper and divide between 2 plates. Put the eggs on top, scatter over the ham and eat straight away.

Braised Ibérico pork with tomatoes, chorizo, thyme and black olives

Pork shoulder is the perfect cut for braising and it's good value for money. This is another recipe that showcases beautiful ingredients from the central area of Spain and how well they combine to create earthy, flavoursome dishes. Serve with *patatas fritas* for a wholesome meal.

Serves 4–6

1kg boned shoulder of pork, ideally Ibérico, cut into 3cm chunks

4 tablespoons olive oil

150ml red wine

2 medium onions, chopped

6 garlic cloves, finely chopped

200g chorizo sausage, skinned and chopped

2 teaspoons sweet *pimentón*

2 tablespoons tomato purée

400g skinned, chopped tomatoes, fresh or canned

300ml chicken stock

leaves from 3 large thyme sprigs

2 tablespoons chopped marjoram or oregano

4 bay leaves

3 tablespoons sherry vinegar

2 teaspoons caster sugar

100g good-quality pitted black olives

sea salt and freshly ground black pepper

1 quantity *patatas fritas* (see page 117), to serve

Season the pork with salt and pepper. Heat 2 tablespoons of the oil in a large, flameproof casserole and sear the pork in batches until nicely browned. Set aside in a bowl. Add the wine to the pan and, as the liquid bubbles up, scrape the base of the pan with a wooden spoon to release all the caramelised juices. Pour over the pork.

Add the remaining oil to the pan with the onions, cover and fry gently for 15 minutes, stirring now and then, until they are very soft and lightly browned. Add the garlic and chorizo and fry for a further 2–3 minutes. Stir in the *pimentón* and cook for 1 minute, then add the tomato purée, tomatoes, chicken stock, thyme leaves, marjoram or oregano and the bay leaves. Stir in the pork and all the juices, season with salt and pepper, cover and simmer gently for 1 hour until the pork is almost tender.

Put the sherry vinegar and caster sugar into a small pan and boil until reduced to about 1 teaspoon. Stir it into the casserole with the olives and simmer uncovered for another 20–30 minutes until the sauce is nicely reduced and the pork is tender. Adjust the seasoning to taste and serve with the *patatas fritas*.

Clear chicken and vegetable soup with roasted garlic croûtes

The bread is very important for this dish – you need a rustic-style loaf with a crusty exterior and densely textured crumb, and lots of flavour. This is classic comfort food for a cold wintery day. The garlic from La Mancha has a subtle sweet flavour that works well with the soup.

Serves 4

2 heads of garlic

2 tablespoons extra virgin olive oil, plus extra to serve (optional)

4 chicken thighs

2 large carrots, sliced

2 leeks, thinly sliced

4 celery sticks, sliced

3 bay leaves

8 black peppercorns

150g smoked pancetta lardons

1 medium onion, halved and thinly sliced

1½ teaspoons sweet *pimentón*

200g vine-ripened tomatoes, skinned, deseeded and chopped

4 x 1cm-thick slices of crusty white bread

sea salt and freshly ground black pepper

Preheat the oven to 200°C/gas mark 6. Remove the outer layer of papery skin from each head of garlic and take a thin slice off the top of each one to expose the cloves. Tear off 2 squares of foil, place a head of garlic into the centre of each one, drizzle each with 1 teaspoon of the olive oil and sprinkle with a little salt. Wrap securely in the foil, place in a small roasting tin and roast for 1 hour until the garlic feels soft when pressed.

Meanwhile, put the chicken thighs into a pan with 1 of the sliced carrots, 1 of the sliced leeks, 1 of the sliced sticks of celery, the bay leaves, peppercorns and 1.2 litres cold water. Bring to the boil, cover and leave to simmer gently for 1 hour.

Strain the stock into a bowl, reserving the chicken thighs but discarding the vegetables. Remove the chicken meat from the bones, discarding the skin, and set aside.

Heat the remaining olive oil in a medium pan, add the pancetta and fry gently until golden. Add the onion and continue to fry over a medium heat until it is soft and lightly golden. Stir in the *pimentón* and fry for a further minute, then stir in the remaining sliced carrot, leek and celery, cover and cook gently for 5–6 minutes. Uncover, add the chicken stock and some seasoning and simmer for 5 minutes until the vegetables are just tender. Stir in the chicken meat and tomatoes and adjust the seasoning to taste.

Lightly toast the slices of bread, then singe them over a gas flame, if you can, for a little extra flavour. Spread each one with some of the roasted garlic purée, drizzle with a little olive oil and sprinkle lightly with some sea salt. Place a slice of toast into the bottom of each of 4 warmed soup plates, ladle the soup on top and serve, drizzled with a little extra olive oil if you wish.

Griddled marinated quail with lentil, chorizo and garlic stew

I have such a vivid memory of seeing quail running through the lentil fields in Extremadura when I was younger. This recipe marries some of the best ingredients of the region – you can tell they have been combined for centuries because they naturally work so well together.

Serves 4

8 quail

For the marinade

4 garlic cloves

2 tablespoons olive oil

3 tablespoons lemon juice

1 teaspoon hot *pimentón*

2 teaspoons cumin seeds, lightly crushed

sea salt and freshly ground black pepper

For the lentil, chorizo and garlic stew

300g green lentils, such as pardina or Puy

4 tablespoons olive oil

300g cooking chorizo sausage, skinned and chopped

100g shallots, finely chopped

8 garlic cloves, thinly sliced

1 large carrot (200g), finely chopped

2 celery sticks, finely chopped

1 tablespoon chopped oregano or marjoram

150ml dry white wine

200g skinned, chopped tomatoes, fresh or canned

150ml good-quality chicken stock

Put the quail breast-side down on a board and cut along either side of the backbone with kitchen scissors and remove. Open up each quail, turn over and press down on the breast bone to make them lie flat.

Use the blade of a large knife to crush the garlic for the marinade to a smooth paste with a little salt. Mix the olive oil, lemon juice, *pimentón*, garlic and crushed cumin seeds in a large shallow dish. Add the quail and rub the marinade well into each bird. Set aside to marinate for 1 hour.

Put the lentils into a pan and cover with cold water. Bring to the boil and simmer for 25–30 minutes, adding 1 teaspoon salt 5 minutes before the end of the cooking time, until just tender but still slightly *al punto* – with a little bite. Drain, reserving the cooking liquid.

For the lentil stew, heat the olive oil in a saucepan over a medium heat. Add the chorizo and fry for 1 minute, stirring. Add the shallots, garlic, carrot and celery, cover and fry gently for 15 minutes until soft and lightly browned. Uncover, add the marjoram or oregano and fry for a further 1 minute, then add the wine and simmer vigorously until it has almost disappeared. Add the tomatoes and chicken stock, bring to the boil and simmer for 5 minutes until the mixture has slightly reduced and thickened. Stir in the cooked lentils and some seasoning to taste and keep hot.

Heat a ridged cast-iron griddle over a high heat until it is smoking hot, then reduce the heat to medium. Season the quail with salt, put them skin-side down onto the griddle and cook for 5–7 minutes on each side until nicely browned and cooked through. Work in batches if necessary. Stir some of the reserved lentil cooking liquid into the lentil stew if it seems a bit dry, and serve with the griddled quail on top.

Confit of pheasant with sautéed red cabbage, raisins and pine nuts

Hunting is a much-loved pastime for the locals and so game in the central regions is abundant. Pheasant shouldn't be too hard to find – ask at your local butcher or visit a farmers' market. The pine nuts from Castile are exceptional and have a sweetness and aroma that transports you to that area. You can use the breast meat of the pheasants with *planchada* beans for a delicious simple supper.

Serves 4

For the pheasant confit

100g coarse sea salt

½ teaspoon coarsely crushed black pepper

leaves from 3 thyme sprigs

6 juniper berries

8 large, plump pheasant legs

1kg duck or goose fat

For the sautéed red cabbage

100g raisins

4 tablespoons Pedro Ximenez sherry vinegar

3 tablespoons olive oil

1 medium onion, halved and thinly sliced

2 garlic cloves, crushed

600g red cabbage, quartered, cored and
   thinly sliced

½ teaspoon ground cumin

½ teaspoon ground coriander

1 tablespoon clear honey

25g pine nuts, toasted

sea salt and freshly ground black pepper

For the pheasant confit, put the salt, pepper, thyme leaves and juniper berries into a food processor and grind them together. Place the pheasant legs skin-side down in a shallow china dish and sprinkle over half of the salt. Turn them over and sprinkle over the rest of the salt. Cover and refrigerate for 4–5 hours.

Preheat the oven to 130°C/gas mark 1. Rub the salt off the pheasant legs and pat them dry. Melt the duck or goose fat in a flameproof casserole in which the legs will fit quite snugly. Add the pheasant legs, making sure they are completely submerged, bring to a simmer, cover with a lid and transfer to the oven. Cook for 1½ hours or until the meat is very tender but not falling off the bone. Remove from the oven and, if using straight away, shake off the excess fat and place the legs skin-side up in a roasting tin.

If not using straight away, refrigerate until the fat is hard, then carefully lift out the legs encased in fat and scrape away and discard (or save for stock) the jelly-like pheasant juices from the base of the pan. Return the legs encased in fat to the pan, place it on the heat and leave until the fat has melted again. Push the pheasant legs under the surface, turn off the heat, leave to cool and refrigerate until needed. Then ease the legs out of the fat, scrape away the excess and put them skin-side up into a roasting tin.

Preheat the oven to 200°C/gas mark 6. Roast the pheasant legs for 15–20 minutes until heated through and the skin is golden brown.

Meanwhile, make the red cabbage. Put the raisins and 3 tablespoons of the sherry vinegar into a small pan and warm gently over a low heat. Remove and set aside. Heat the oil in a medium pan. Add the onion and fry for 5 minutes until soft and lightly browned. Add the garlic and fry for 2 minutes, then add the cabbage and stir-fry for 5 minutes. Add the cumin, coriander and some seasoning, lower the heat, cover and leave to cook for 8–10 minutes, giving it a stir every now and then, until tender.

Stir the vinegar-soaked raisins and the honey into the cabbage, and cook for a further 2 minutes. Stir in the remaining vinegar and some salt and pepper to taste, then stir in the pine nuts. Serve with the pheasant.

Venison, red wine and chestnut stew

When we were filming with Rick Stein in Extremadura, we went to Marques de Valduza to hunt deer, but we didn't end up shooting any and so settled for a delicious *ajo blanco* soup instead! Extremadura is abundant with chestnut trees and they are used in many different recipes. The nuttiness goes well with the gamey flavour of the venison. A *tempranillo* from the area would be perfect to use as your red wine in the recipe and to drink with it.

Serves 4–6

1kg stewing venison, preferably from the leg or haunch

25g plain flour

5 tablespoons olive oil

4 tablespoons sherry vinegar

150g pancetta or dry-cured streaky bacon, cut into short fat strips

1 medium onion, halved and thinly sliced

4 garlic cloves, crushed

300ml game or beef stock

200ml robust red wine, such as *tempranillo*

1 teaspoon tomato purée

100ml sweet sherry, such as Oloroso

leaves from 3 large thyme sprigs

1 teaspoon juniper berries, lightly crushed

2 tablespoons clear honey

200g baby onions, peeled

200g cooked, peeled chestnuts

sea salt and freshly ground black pepper

1 quantity *patatas fritas* (see page 117) or Olive Oil Mash (see page 33), to serve

Cut the venison into 4cm pieces. Coat them lightly in the flour, reserving the excess. Heat 2 tablespoons of the oil in a large, flameproof casserole over a medium-high heat. Brown the venison in batches, spooning it into a bowl as each batch is done.

Pour away the excess oil from the casserole, add the vinegar to the pan and scrape the base with a wooden spoon as the liquid bubbles, to release all the caramelised juices. Pour over the venison in the bowl.

Add another tablespoon of the oil and the pancetta to the casserole and fry for 2 minutes until lightly golden. Remove with a slotted spoon and add to the venison. Add another tablespoon of the oil and the onion and fry for 7–8 minutes, stirring frequently, until soft and richly golden. Add the garlic and cook for 2 minutes. Stir in any remaining flour, followed by the game or beef stock, red wine, tomato purée, sherry, thyme leaves, juniper berries and honey. Bring to the boil, stirring. Return the venison, pancetta and all the juices to the casserole, season with salt and pepper and stir well. Cover and leave to simmer gently for 1 hour.

Meanwhile, heat the remaining oil in a small pan, add the baby onions and fry, shaking the pan every now and then, until they are nicely browned all over. Uncover the casserole and stir in the baby onions and the chestnuts. Simmer for another 25 minutes until the meat is tender. Leave the casserole uncovered if the liquid needs to reduce and thicken a little more. Serve with *patatas fritas* or olive oil mash.

Hunter's rice with rabbit and wild herbs

It is best to prepare the rabbit in advance so that you can make a stock from the bones. In my area, there used to be many more hares than rabbits (although it's the opposite these days), so this dish was made with hare and ingredients that the hunter would have readily. Here we use farmed rabbit, but if you're lucky enough to get a wild rabbit the cooking time will be about 20 minutes longer. If neither is available, you can substitute chicken.

Serves 4–6

pinch of saffron strands

1 litre rabbit or chicken stock

175g dwarf green beans, trimmed

1 farmed rabbit (or 750g chicken), cut into small pieces through the bone

3 tablespoons olive oil

1 medium onion, finely chopped

4 garlic cloves, finely chopped

½ teaspoon sweet *pimentón* (optional)

¼ teaspoon crushed dried chillies

300g vine-ripened tomatoes, skinned and chopped

leaves from 2 large thyme sprigs

leaves from a 10cm rosemary sprig, chopped

leaves from 2 large wild oregano sprigs, chopped

6 small bay leaves

400g paella rice (preferably Calasparra)

280g jar artichokes in olive oil, drained and cut into quarters

sea salt and freshly ground black pepper

Bring a pan of well-salted water to the boil. Shake the saffron around in a hot, dry frying pan for a few seconds, then tip into a mortar and grind to a fine powder. Transfer the saffron powder to a pan, add the stock and bring to the boil, then remove from the heat and set aside. Drop the green beans into the boiling water and cook for 3 minutes. Drain, refresh under cold water and set aside.

Season the rabbit (or chicken) pieces with salt and pepper. Heat the olive oil in a 38cm paella pan or large, deep frying pan over a medium heat, add the meat and fry until golden brown all over. Lift onto a plate and set aside.

Add the onion to the pan and fry for 6–7 minutes until soft and lightly golden. Add the garlic, *pimentón* (if using) and the crushed dried chillies and fry for 1 minute. Add the tomatoes and cook for 2 minutes. Stir in the herbs and cook for a further 2 minutes. Add the stock and bring to the boil. Taste the stock and season with salt and plenty of pepper.

Pour in the rice and stir so that it is evenly distributed in the pan. Place the rabbit (or chicken) pieces around the pan with the artichokes and shake the pan gently so the pieces bed down into the rice. Scatter over the green beans and leave to simmer vigorously for 6 minutes. Then lower the heat and leave to cook undisturbed for 14–15 minutes, until all the liquid has been absorbed and the rice is *al punto* – still with a little bite. Turn off the heat, cover the pan with a clean cloth and leave it to rest for 5 minutes before serving.

Slow-cooked beans with partridge, bacon and garlic

This recipe originated in Castile, but the combination of beans and partridge is used all over Spain. The beans and the partridge have different cooking times, so for this dish it is better to cook them separately. My mother used to prepare a recipe like this after my brother and I had been shooting the first partridge in the autumn, but I have added some pancetta to bring a bit of fattiness and therefore extra flavour. This is a great dinner-party dish for the autumn months.

Serves 4

7 tablespoons olive oil
2 medium onions, chopped
1 small head of garlic, separated into cloves and finely chopped
¼ teaspoon crushed dried chillies
400g dried white beans, such as *alubia planchada*, soaked in water overnight
1 bay leaf
4 oven-ready partridges (or 6 quail)
200g streaky bacon or pancetta, diced
2 green peppers, deseeded and thinly sliced
1 teaspoon sweet *pimentón*
150ml dry white wine
750ml good-quality chicken stock
sea salt and freshly ground black pepper
1 tablespoon chopped flat-leaf parsley, to serve

For the slow-cooked beans, heat 3 tablespoons of the oil in a large saucepan, add 1 of the chopped onions, half the chopped garlic and the crushed dried chillies, cover and fry gently for 10 minutes until soft and lightly golden. Drain and rinse the beans, add them to the pan with the bay leaf and cover with 1 litre cold water. Bring to a gentle simmer, reduce the heat to low, part-cover and leave to cook for 2 hours until the liquid has reduced and almost disappeared and the beans are very tender.

Meanwhile, cut the partridges in half lengthways, through the backbone and breastbone, using kitchen scissors and clean them well of any stray feathers or bits of gut. Season all over with salt and pepper.

Heat the remaining oil in a flameproof casserole over a medium heat. Add the partridge halves and fry them until golden brown all over. Lift them onto a plate and set aside.

Add the bacon or pancetta to the pan and fry for 2 minutes until lightly golden. Add the remaining chopped onion and garlic and the green peppers and cook for 5 minutes until soft. Stir in the *pimentón*, followed by the wine, and leave it to bubble away until reduced by half. Return the partridges to the pan with the stock, bring back to a simmer, part-cover and cook over a low heat for 40–50 minutes, depending on the size of the birds, until they are quite tender and the liquid has reduced by about half.

Strip the meat off the bones if you wish (simply to make this dish slightly easier to eat). Stir the beans into the partridge stew, adjust the seasoning to taste and bring back to a simmer. Ladle into 4 warmed shallow bowls and serve sprinkled with the chopped parsley.

Barbecued lamb with honey, mustard, garlic and rosemary

The honey in the marinade makes the surface of the lamb caramelise to give a fantastic flavour, which contrasts so well with the beautifully tender pink meat inside. We couldn't find neck fillets in *La Boqueria*, the famous food market in Barcelona, as they don't butcher there in the same way, so we used a seam-boned leg of lamb instead. This is wonderful served with the lentil salad on page 132 or the 'poor man's potatoes' on page 109.

Serves 4

4 x 225g lamb neck fillets or 1 small leg
    of lamb, seam-boned

For the marinade

3 fat garlic cloves

4 tablespoons clear honey

1 tablespoon wholegrain mustard

leaves from 2 x 10cm rosemary sprigs,
    finely chopped

2 tablespoons olive oil

1½ tablespoons lemon juice

sea salt and freshly ground black pepper

For the marinade, use the blade of a large knife to crush the garlic to a smooth paste with a little salt. Mix together the honey, mustard, garlic, rosemary, olive oil, lemon juice and some pepper in a shallow dish. Add the lamb fillets or boned lamb, turn them over in the mixture to coat well and leave to marinate for at least 1 hour.

Preheat your barbecue to medium-high. Lift the lamb fillets out of the marinade and shake off the excess. Season with salt and a little more pepper. Barbecue the lamb fillets for 5 minutes on each side, basting once or twice with the leftover marinade, until nicely browned on the outside and slightly pink in the centre. Some pieces of the boned lamb will take a little longer, so barbecue until the centre of the meat registers 60°C on a meat thermometer. Lift the fillets onto a board, wrap tightly in foil and leave them to rest for 4–5 minutes. Then slice thickly and serve straight away.

Chargrilled leg of lamb with a fennel and lentil salad

This is a wonderful recipe to barbecue, but you can get the same effect by starting it off on a large ridged griddle to give it a good colour and smoky flavour, then transfering to the oven in a roasting dish to finish it off. A winter alternative to fennel is radicchio, giving an extra bite to the dish.

Serves 6

1 x 2.5kg leg of lamb, butterflied

sea salt

For the marinade

6 tablespoons olive oil

leaves from 1 large rosemary sprig, finely chopped

2 large garlic cloves, crushed

finely grated zest and juice of 1 small lemon

½ teaspoon coarsely crushed black peppercorns

For the fennel and lentil salad

1 large fennel bulb

300g green lentils, such as pardina or Puy

6 tablespoons extra virgin olive oil

finely grated zest of ½ lemon and 2 tablespoons lemon juice

150g good-quality black olives, pitted

2 tablespoons chopped fennel herb or fronds

For the marinade, mix the oil, rosemary, garlic, lemon zest and juice, pepper and some of the salt together in a large shallow dish. Add the lamb, turn it over a few times to coat well, then cover and leave to marinate at room temperature for at least 1 hour or in the fridge overnight.

The next day, if you are barbecuing your lamb, preheat the barbecue to high. Alternatively, preheat the oven to 200°C/gas mark 6. Meanwhile, make the salad. Thinly slice the fennel bulb on a mandolin, drop the slices into a large bowl of iced water and leave in the fridge to crisp up. Put the lentils into a pan, cover by 5cm with cold water, bring to the boil and simmer for about 25–30 minutes or until just cooked but still a little *al punto* (with a little bite), adding 1 teaspoon salt 5 minutes before the end of cooking. Meanwhile, whisk together the olive oil, lemon juice, lemon zest and some salt and pepper to taste. Drain the lentils well, tip into a bowl and stir in the lemon dressing. Leave to cool.

Season the lamb with salt, place skin-side down, on the barbecue and cook for 12–15 minutes on each side, moving it around now and then to avoid any flare-ups. (Alternatively, preheat a large ridged griddle over a high heat, reduce the heat slightly and griddle the lamb for 5–7 minutes on each side. Then transfer to a roasting tin and roast in the oven for 20–25 minutes.) The meat is cooked to medium when it registers 60°C at its thickest part. Lift it onto a board, wrap loosely in foil and leave to rest for 5–10 minutes.

To finish the salad, drain the sliced fennel and dry it well in a salad spinner or on a clean tea towel. Stir the fennel into the lentils with the black olives, fennel herb and a little more seasoning to taste. Carve the lamb across into slices and serve with the salad.

Spiced beef and potato fritters

When I started researching this book, I asked my lovely sister Isabel to find me Spanish cookbooks that had a Jewish influence, and I found this recipe, created by the Jews from north Extremadura. It looks rather elaborate, but it is worth the effort because the fritters taste amazing.

Makes 14 fritters

1kg floury potatoes, such as Maris Piper

1 egg, beaten

olive oil, for shallow-frying

50g fresh white breadcrumbs

sea salt and freshly ground black pepper

green salad, to serve

For the filling

1 medium onion, finely chopped

3 tablespoons olive oil

350g lean minced beef (or lamb)

seeds from 4 green cardamom pods

1 teaspoon cumin seeds

2 teaspoon coriander seeds

1 teaspoon ground cinnamon

½ teaspoon ground allspice

½ teaspoon sweet pimentón

freshly grated nutmeg

3 tablespoons chopped flat-leaf parsley

For the filling, fry the onion in the olive oil for 10 minutes until soft and lightly golden. Add the minced beef and fry for 2–3 minutes, breaking up any lumps with a spoon as it browns. Put the cardamom, cumin and coriander seeds into a spice grinder and grind to a fine powder. Add to the minced beef mixture with the cinnamon, allspice, pimentón, salt, pepper and 200ml water. Simmer gently, stirring now and then, until all the liquid has evaporated. Tip into a sieve set over a bowl and drain away the excess oil. Return to the pan, stir in the nutmeg and parsley and adjust the seasoning if necessary. Allow to cool.

Meanwhile, cut the potatoes into large chunks, put into a pan of well-salted water, bring to the boil and cook for 20 minutes or until tender. Drain well, leave until the steam dies down, then return to the pan and mash until smooth. Stir in the beaten egg and some salt and pepper to taste. Leave until cool enough to handle.

Lightly oil your hands and shape a tangerine-sized piece (65g) of mashed potato into a flat 10cm disc. Put a tablespoon of the meat mixture into the centre and wrap the potato around it to form a ball. Seal any gaps, then flatten gently into a 7cm pattie. Repeat with the remaining filling and mash. The patties can be prepared up to this point in advance.

Heat 1cm of olive oil in a large frying pan over a medium heat to 170°C (use a cooking thermometer). Coat half of the fritters in the breadcrumbs, add them to the pan and fry for 5 minutes on each side until crisp and golden. Lift onto a tray lined with kitchen paper and keep warm while you coat and cook the remainder. Serve with a lightly dressed green leaf salad.

Pan-fried lamb's brains on toast with lettuce and walnut oil dressing

My mother used to cook me lamb's brains, just blanched and deep-fried in a simple batter, served with toasted bread. Sometimes we would have them in scrambled egg – they were delicious. You can find lamb's brains in speciality butchers.

Serves 4

2 lamb's brains

4 tablespoons olive oil

1 tablespoon cold-pressed walnut oil

2½ teaspoons good-quality white wine vinegar

4 large or 8 small slices of brown walnut bread, 1cm thick

25g butter

½ oak leaf lettuce, broken into leaves

25g walnut pieces, lightly toasted

sea salt and freshly ground black pepper

Soak the lamb's brains in cold water for 24 hours, changing the water now and then. Bring 2.25 litres water to the boil with 1 tablespoon salt. Split each brain into 2 lobes, add them to the boiling water, bring back to the boil, then remove from the heat and leave them to cool in the liquid. This can be done in advance. Remove the membrane and any veins from the brains. Slice each lobe lengthways into 3 slices.

Whisk 2 tablespoons of the olive oil, the walnut oil and vinegar together in a small bowl and season to taste with salt and pepper.

Toast the slices of walnut bread and put onto each plate. Put half the butter and 1 tablespoon of the remaining oil into a large frying pan over a high heat and, when the butter foams, add half of the lamb's brain slices, season lightly and fry for 1 minute on each side. Divide between 2 of the slices of toast. Repeat with the remaining butter, oil and brains. Toss 1 tablespoon of the salad dressing through the lettuce leaves and scatter them around the plates. Sprinkle with the toasted walnuts, drizzle the remaining dressing over the plates and serve.

Liver with sweet caramelised onions and slow-cooked grapes

Offal has been popular in the central regions of Spain since the time of Don Quixote and before. It was used because of poverty and necessity. The combination of the earthy flavour of the liver and the sweetness of the onions and grapes is delicious. Moscatel grapes would be really lovely in this recipe.

Serves 4

500g small, seedless red grapes

5 tablespoons olive oil

4 medium onions, halved and thinly sliced

400g lamb's liver, cut into 8 slices, 1cm thick

3 tablespoons sweet sherry, such as Pedro Ximenez

2 teaspoons Pedro Ximenez sherry vinegar

sea salt and freshly ground black pepper

Preheat the oven to 200°C/gas mark 6. Spread the grapes out on a non-stick baking tray. Roast for 25–30 minutes, shaking the tray now and then to prevent them from sticking. Reduce the oven temperature to 130°C/gas mark 1 and roast for a further 40–45 minutes until shrivelled, sticky and sweet. Remove and set aside.

Heat 2 tablespoons of the oil in a large frying pan, add the sliced onions, cover and cook over a medium heat, stirring now and then, for about 15–20 minutes until soft and nicely caramelised. Season and set aside.

Season the lamb's liver on both sides. Heat the remaining oil in a large frying pan over a medium heat. Add the liver slices and cook for about 20–30 seconds on each side. Lift the lamb's liver onto a warmed plate. Pour away the excess oil from the pan, add the sherry and sherry vinegar and scrape the base of the pan with a wooden spoon as the liquid bubbles to release all the caramelised juices. Season to taste. Stir in the slow-cooked grapes and warm through quickly.

To serve, spoon the caramelised onions onto warmed plates and put the liver on top. Spoon over the sauce and grapes and serve.

Orange, almond and pine nut tartlets

These little tarts are so moreish. The flavours combine to create a not-too-sweet pastry that can be savoured any time of the day. They are perfect for a dinner-party dessert or warm from the oven for a teatime treat.

Makes 8 individual tartlets or 1 x 23cm tart

For the pastry

225g plain flour, plus extra for dusting

pinch of salt

65g icing sugar

125g chilled butter, cut into small pieces

finely grated zest of ½ large orange

1 large egg yolk

4 teaspoons orange juice

For the filling

175g butter, softened

175g caster sugar

finely grated zest of 2 small oranges

2 large free-range eggs

40g self-raising flour

175g ground almonds

75g pine nuts, toasted

40g chopped mixed peel, plus extra to decorate

4 tablespoons peel-free marmalade, to glaze

For the pastry, sift the flour, salt and icing sugar into a food processor. Add the butter and orange zest and process briefly until the mixture resembles fine breadcrumbs. Beat the egg yolk briefly with the orange juice. Tip the crumbed mixture into a bowl, stir in the egg yolk and orange mixture and bring the dough together into a ball. Turn out onto a lightly floured surface and knead briefly until smooth. Chill for 15 minutes, then remove from the fridge and, if making individual tartlets, cut into 8 even-sized pieces. Thinly roll out the pastry and use to line either 8 lightly buttered 10cm tartlet cases with sides 4cm deep or loose-based 23cm tart tin with sides 4cm deep. Refrigerate for 20 minutes.

Put a baking sheet on the middle shelf of the oven and preheat it to 200°C/gas mark 6. Line the pastry case(s) with foil and a thin layer of baking beans and bake for 15 minutes. Remove the foil and beans and bake for a further 3 minutes or until the pastry is crisp and golden brown. Remove from the oven and set aside. Reduce the oven temperature to 170°C/gas mark 3.

For the filling, beat the butter, sugar and orange zest together in a bowl until light and fluffy. Gradually beat in the eggs, adding the flour with the final addition. Fold in the ground almonds, pine nuts and chopped mixed peel. Spoon the mixture into the pastry case(s) and smooth over the tops. Bake in the centre of the oven for 25–30 minutes for the individual tarts, or 35–40 minutes for the large tart, until puffed up and golden and a skewer, inserted into the centre, comes away clean. Remove the tart(s) from the oven and allow to cool for 10 minutes.

Meanwhile, warm the marmalade with 2 teaspoons water in a small pan. Brush the tart(s) generously with the marmalade, scatter with a little extra chopped mixed peel and serve warm or cold.

Grilled figs with goat's cheese, honey and walnuts

This recipe reminds me of my father because he has figs and walnuts in his garden and makes honey. We used to get goat's curd from the local farmer, which was so delicious. Now it is harder to get, so I have used a soft goat's cheese instead.

Serves 4

40g walnut pieces
8 large fresh figs
100g soft rindless goat's cheese, thinly sliced
3 tablespoons clear honey
4 large mint leaves, finely shredded

Preheat the grill to medium-high. Spread the walnuts on a baking tray and carefully toast them for a minute or two until lightly golden. Remove and leave to go cold.

Cut a deep cross into the top of each fig, about two-thirds of the way down to the base, and then give them a gentle squeeze to open them up slightly like a flower. Divide the goat's cheese between each fig and place them on a baking tray. Grill for 3–4 minutes until the figs are soft and the cheese is bubbling and lightly golden.

Lift the figs onto plates and drizzle a little honey over each one. Sprinkle with the walnuts and mint before serving.

Velvety chocolate pots with marrons glacés

The most popular way of eating chocolate in Spain is in *churros con chocolate*, deep-fried lengths of flour and water paste (they are like doughnuts), sometimes dusted in sugar, dipped into small cups of very thick hot chocolate. But I love chocolate in any way, and these little pots are my idea of heaven after a good meal. Chestnuts are very popular in Extremadura and so I make this dessert for my sister when I go and visit.

Makes 6

6 marrons glacés
100ml whole milk
300ml double cream
30g caster sugar
180g good-quality dark chocolate (at least 70% cocoa solids)
1½ teaspoons vanilla extract
1 large free-range egg, beaten

Preheat the oven to 130°C/gas mark 1 and put a kettleful of water on to boil. Cut 6 of the marrons glacés into small thin pieces. Divide evenly between six 120ml heatproof pots or ramekins of 120ml capacity and put them into a small roasting tin. Slice the remaining marrons glacés and set aside.

Put the milk, cream and sugar into a small pan and bring slowly to the boil, stirring once or twice to dissolve the sugar. Meanwhile, break the chocolate into a small mixing bowl. As soon as the milk mixture starts to bubble around the edge of the pan, remove from the heat, leave for 1 minute to cool slightly, then pour onto the chocolate and stir until smooth. Stir in the vanilla extract and beaten egg. Strain the mixture into a jug and pour equally into the pots.

Pour hot (but not boiling) water from the kettle into the roasting tin to come halfway up the sides of the pots. Carefully slide the tin into the oven and cook for 15 minutes until the pots are almost set but still have a slight wobble in the centre. Remove the tray from the oven, take the pots out of the water and leave them to cool and set at room temperature, then serve.

Walnut and orange blossom honey tart

This is a perfect tart to make in advance as it lasts for 2 or 3 days easily. I always use orange blossom honey to give a fruity, floral flavour to the tart. You could serve it with ice cream as dessert or on its own for tea.

Serves 8–10 (makes 1 x 23cm tart)

For the pastry

175g plain flour

pinch of salt

50g icing sugar

90g chilled butter, cut into small pieces

finely grated zest of ½ lemon

1 medium egg yolk

1 tablespoon cold water

For the filling

75g unsalted butter

90g light muscovado sugar

125g orange blossom honey

150ml double cream

1½ tablespoons lemon juice

1 large egg, beaten

200g walnut halves

For the pastry, sift the flour, salt and icing sugar into a food processor. Add the butter and lemon zest and process briefly until the mixture resembles fine breadcrumbs. Beat the egg yolk briefly with the water. Tip the crumbed mixture into a bowl, stir in the egg yolk mixture and bring the dough together into a ball. Turn out onto a lightly floured surface and knead briefly until smooth. Chill for 15 minutes, then remove from the fridge, thinly roll out into a disc and use to line a 23cm, loose-based tart tin with sides 2.5cm deep. Refrigerate for 20 minutes.

Put a baking sheet on the middle shelf of the oven and preheat it to 200°C/gas mark 6. Line the pastry case with foil and a thin layer of baking beans and bake for 15–20 minutes until the edges are biscuit-coloured. Remove the foil and beans and bake for another 5–7 minutes or until the base of the case is crisp and golden brown. Remove and set aside. Reduce the oven temperature to 180°C/gas mark 4.

For the filling, melt the butter in a medium pan over a low heat. Add the sugar and honey and stir gently until the sugar has dissolved. Then raise the heat and simmer vigorously for 4 minutes. Add the cream (be careful as it will splutter a little) and boil for a further 3 minutes. Stir in the lemon juice. Remove from the heat and leave the mixture to cool until just warm, then stir in the beaten egg.

Arrange the walnut halves over the base of the pastry case in an even layer and pour over the honey and cream mixture. Bake for 30–35 minutes until the filling is set and golden brown. Serve warm, cut into wedges.

THE SOUTH

THE SOUTH: INTRODUCTION

El Andalus was the name the Muslims gave to the southern part of Spain that they conquered and governed for over 700 years and Andalusia is derived from the Arabic name for their mighty kingdom. It is now the largest of the country's 17 autonomous regions and world famous for its flamenco, fiestas and bull fights. The legacy of the Moorish occupation is very much apparent in Andalusia's architecture and culinary traditions, including many exotic ingredients – among them mint, coriander, cinnamon, olives, citrus fruits including the bitter Seville oranges, figs, dates, aubergines, sugarcane, rice and vines – and Arabic cooking styles, such as the use of dried fruits and honey in savoury as well as sweet recipes.

Andalusia is associated in my mind with family holidays, particularly the area around Puerto de Santa María. I can still recall the long trips from Talaván in Extremadura to Cadiz, which took 6 overpoweringly hot hours travelling in the back of a Citroen 2CV. Now, thankfully, the journey is a lot quicker, only 3 hours.

I visit Andalusia, not only for my vacations, but for my work. The heat and long hours of sunshine make this blessed region the source of great ingredients – seemingly exotic fruit and vegetables, and a vast array of olives and oils – that I use in my kitchen and they feature in many of the traditional recipes that I have on the menu in my restaurants and certainly in my books. Being a chef offers me the perfect excuse to visit the south whenever I can and stroll through Seville when the orange trees are in bloom, to visit the Alhambra of Granada or the mosque at Córdoba, witness the horse races along the beach at Sanlúcar de Barrameda, or spend summer nights eating freshly fried fish on a terrace or enjoy a lazy afternoon with friends moving from one tapas bar to another.

One of my passions is sherry, the wines of Jerez. There is always a bottle in my kitchen – for drinking and cooking. Many people ask me which sherry wines I use for cooking, and my response is very simple: Manzanilla and Fino, the lightest and driest of the sherry styles, are used in the same way as white wine, while the darker, richer styles such as Palo Cortado and Oloroso can be used in the same way as red wine. Adding sherry to a dish imparts a certain flavour and a very different aroma, which derive from the yeast in the wine. The darkest and sweetest of all sherries, which has been described as 'Christmas pudding in a glass', is Pedro Ximenez, an irresistible accompaniment to a dessert, but not only to drink with it – try adding a generous spoonful to good vanilla ice cream: simple but amazing.

Crisp, deep-fried aubergine fritters with honey

This is another really good, easy tapas dish that sells very quickly in 'José'. The delicious, subtle flavour of the soft aubergine comes through the crispy coating and the sticky honey make this a heavenly dish.

Serves 4–6

300g aubergines, cut into 7–8mm-thick slices

110g plain flour

5 tablespoons olive oil, plus extra for
   deep-frying

150ml cold water

2 free-range egg whites

clear honey, for drizzling

fine sea salt

Sprinkle the aubergine slices lightly on both sides with salt and set aside for 30 minutes. Sift the flour into a bowl, make a well in the centre and add the oil and the water. Gradually beat together to make a smooth batter. Set aside to rest, along with the aubergines.

Pat the aubergine slices dry with kitchen paper. Pour 1cm of olive oil into a large deep frying pan and heat it to 180°C.

Whisk the egg whites into soft peaks and fold them into the batter. Dip the aubergine slices, a few at a time, into the batter, add them to the hot oil and deep-fry for 1 minute on each side until crisp and golden. Leave to drain briefly on kitchen paper and serve immediately while they are still hot and crisp, drizzled generously with the honey.

Sweet-and-sour Moorish aubergines with chilli, garlic and mint

I always have a call from my friend Tony in Maltby Street market, when the first aubergines have come in. I love to cook this recipe with those first small aubergines, mixing the Moorish herbs and spices with the smoky-tasting vegetables. This recipe is great for lunch or as a starter.

Serves 4

500g small, thin aubergines

200ml red wine vinegar

40g caster sugar

6 tablespoons extra virgin olive oil

4 garlic cloves, finely chopped

1 medium-hot red chilli, deseeded and finely chopped

2 tablespoons chopped mint, plus a few small whole leaves to garnish

sea salt and freshly ground black pepper

Halve the aubergines lengthways (or cut into 1cm-thick slices if you can find only large ones). Sprinkle lightly on both sides with salt and set aside for 30 minutes.

Put the red wine vinegar and sugar into a small pan and boil until reduced to 50ml. Remove from the heat and set aside. Put 2 tablespoons of the olive oil and the garlic into a small pan and place it over a medium-low heat. As soon as the garlic begins to sizzle, add the red chilli and cook until the garlic is very lightly golden. Stir into the vinegar mixture and season to taste with salt and pepper.

Heat a ridged cast-iron griddle over a high heat until smoking hot, then reduce the heat to medium. Pat the aubergines dry with kitchen paper. Brush a few slices at a time with the remaining oil, place on the griddle and cook for 3 minutes on each side until browned and tender. Transfer each batch to a shallow serving dish as they are ready.

Stir the chopped mint into the dressing and spoon it over the aubergines. Scatter over a few baby mint leaves and serve warm.

Warm potato soup with prawns, eggs and bacalao

This is an unusual but very delicious soup, also known as *sopa de huevos* (egg soup) because it is made from mayonnaise. It is thinned down with the potato cooking water or stock, flavoured with vinegar, and traditionally garnished with diced cooked egg white and potatoes, small prawns and some flaked white fish or *bacalao* (salt cod). It's also good served with clams. The flavour will entirely depend on the olive oil that you use for the mayonnaise, so use the very best that you can find. This soup is quite rich and is therefore usually served only in small portions.

Serves 4

150g piece *bacalao* (salt cod), soaked in
water for at least 24 hours (see page 44)

2 large free-range eggs

250g waxy potatoes, such as Desirée

175g cooked peeled small prawns

sea salt

chopped flat-leaf parsley, to garnish

For the mayonnaise

2 large egg yolks

1 tablespoon sherry vinegar

250ml really good-quality olive oil

First make the mayonnaise. Put the egg yolks into a large mixing bowl, add 2 teaspoons of the vinegar and a good pinch of salt and very gradually whisk in the olive oil until you have a smooth, thick mayonnaise. Cover and set aside.

Put the soaked *bacalao* into a pan, cover with cold water and bring to the boil over a medium heat. Turn off the heat, cover and leave for 10 minutes. Then lift the fish onto a plate and, when it is cool enough to handle, flake the fish, discarding the skin and any bones. Cover and set aside.

Hard-boil the eggs for 9 minutes. Meanwhile, cut the potatoes into 1.5cm dice. Put them into a pan with 600ml cold water and 1 teaspoon salt. Bring to the boil, cover and simmer for 3–4 minutes until they are just tender. Drain the potatoes, reserving the cooking water. Leave to cool slightly. Drain the hard-boiled eggs, cover with cold water and leave to cool. Then peel and cut into small dice.

Whisk 400ml of the potato cooking water into the mayonnaise, pour the mixture into a large pan and stir over a low heat, as you would for a custard, until the mixture thickens and lightly coats the back of the spoon. Take care not to let it boil. Stir in the remaining sherry vinegar and season to taste with salt. Stir in the potatoes, flaked *bacalao* and prawns and continue to heat gently for a further 3–4 minutes, again taking care not to let it boil, until everything has heated through.

Ladle the soup into 4 small warmed bowls and sprinkle with chopped parsley. Serve straight away.

Spicy vegetable and chorizo pisto with eggs

This is a late summer dish that you could make to use up a glut of courgettes and tomatoes. I've added chorizo to the classic *pisto* to make it more robust, but you could always leave it out and enjoy this as a great vegetarian dish, just use a little more *pimentón* for flavour. I've included cumin to give a Moorish influence to the dish.

Serves 2

4 tablespoons olive oil

1 large onion, halved and chopped

1 red pepper, deseeded and diced

2 garlic cloves, finely chopped

1 teaspoon ground cumin

½ teaspoon crushed dried chillies

300g aubergine, cut into 2cm pieces

200g courgettes, cut into 2cm pieces

400g skinned, chopped tomatoes, fresh or canned

4 large free-range eggs

pinch of hot *pimentón*

sea salt and freshly ground black pepper

Heat the oil in a large frying pan over a medium heat. Add the onion and red pepper, cover and cook gently for 7–8 minutes until soft and lightly golden. Uncover, stir in the garlic, cumin and crushed dried chillies and cook for 1 minute. Stir in the aubergine, re-cover and cook for 4 minutes until beginning to soften, then stir in the courgettes, season with salt and cook for another 4 minutes. Stir in the tomatoes, 150ml water and some salt and pepper and simmer for 7–8 minutes until all the vegetables are tender and the sauce has reduced and thickened slightly.

Break the eggs on top of the mixture and sprinkle them with some *pimentón* and a little salt. Cover the pan with a tight-fitting lid and simmer gently for 5 minutes or until the eggs are set to your liking. Serve with fresh crusty bread.

Salmorejo-style tomato soup with hard-boiled eggs, olives and crisp-fried ham

This is a rich, thick and creamy chilled bread soup made without water, which relies on the juice from lots of skinned fresh tomatoes. It is usually served garnished with Serrano ham, which I like to crisp up to add texture, and chopped hard-boiled eggs, but I also serve it from time to time topped with some flaked, good-quality, olive-oil-preserved tuna (see page 158) in place of the crisp-fried ham. *Salmorejo* is typically found in Cordoba, but is enjoyed throughout Spain.

Serves 6–8

340g slightly stale country-style bread, crusts removed (to give 225g crustless white bread)

1kg ripe and juicy vine-ripened tomatoes, skinned

3 garlic cloves, crushed

pinch of sugar (only if your tomatoes lack sweetness)

150ml good-quality olive oil, plus 1 tablespoon, and extra to serve

2 tablespoons sherry vinegar

2 large free-range eggs

6–8 thin slices of Serrano ham

50g good-quality green or black pitted olives, quartered lengthways

sea salt

Break the bread into a bowl and sprinkle with 250ml water. Leave to soak for at least 30 minutes. Meanwhile, quarter the tomatoes and scoop out the seeds into a sieve set over another bowl. Roughly chop the flesh and rub the juices from the seeds through the sieve. Discard the seeds.

Put the tomato flesh and juices into a liquidiser with the garlic and sugar (if using) and blend until smooth. Squeeze as much water as you can from the bread, add the bread to the liquidiser and blend once more, then, with the motor still running, gradually pour in 150ml of the oil, the vinegar and 1½ teaspoons salt. The mixture should be thick but not stiff. Pour into a bowl, cover and chill for at least 2 hours. Chill 4 small soup bowls.

Shortly before serving, lower the eggs into a pan of boiling water and cook for 9 minutes. Drain, cover with cold water, and, when they are cold, peel off the shells and chop both eggs roughly into small pieces.

Heat the remaining tablespoon of oil in a large frying pan over a medium heat. Add 2 slices of ham side by side and fry for about 30 seconds on each side until crisp and lightly golden. Lift onto kitchen paper to drain and cool. Repeat with the remaining ham. Once it is cold, crumble into small pieces.

To serve, spoon the soup into the chilled bowls and garnish with the chopped egg, crisp ham and olives. Drizzle over a little more olive oil and serve straight away while it is still cold.

Prawns baked in salt with anis and fennel herb mayonnaise

Whenever I visit Huelva, on the south Andalucian coast, I always go to a restaurant called Casa Machaquito in Islantilla and have *langostinos* (large king prawns) baked in salt. Those prawns are caught in the area and can cost as much £150 a kilo! Their flavour is indescribable – they are so good and taste so sweet. The casing of salt seals in the flavour of the prawns and enhances the taste of the sea, without making them at all salty. I like to add a few fennel seeds to the salt mixture to give extra flavour and then echo this in some mayonnaise, flavoured with anis and fennel herb, for dipping. A delicious dish for a special occasion.

Serves 4

1 large egg white

2.5kg coarse rock salt

4 tablespoons fennel seeds, lightly crushed

20 large raw unpeeled prawns (as large as you can find or as expensive as you can afford)

To serve

150ml Olive Oil Mayonnaise (see page 227), made without the mustard

1½ teaspoons anis or Pernod

1 tablespoon chopped fennel herb

Preheat the oven to 200°C/gas mark 6. Put the egg white into a bowl and whisk until it forms soft peaks. Stir in the rock salt and crushed fennel seeds and then spread half of the mixture in a 1.5cm-thick, even layer over the base of a large roasting tin.

Lay the prawns side by side on top of the salt and cover with the remaining mixture, ensuring that the prawns are completely covered and there are no gaps. Bake in the oven for 8 minutes, by which time the prawns should be cooked through. However, if they are very thick and meaty, give them an extra couple of minutes.

Remove the tin from the oven and break open the now hard salt crust. Lift the prawns onto a serving plate. Stir the anis and fennel herb into the mayonnaise and serve with the prawns.

Tuna confit with potato salad, roasted red peppers and capers

The tuna from Huelva is fished in the centuries-old way called *almadraba*, where the fishermen use stretched maze-like nets to catch it. Always use a nice thick piece of tuna for the confit so it doesn't cook through too quickly and become dry and tough. And I like to use lemon in this salad and the confit to add an acidity to cut through the tuna. This recipe makes more tuna confit than is needed so store any left over in the fridge, covered in olive oil, for up to 30 days.

Serves 6–8

1 x 500g piece tuna loin, cut 4–5cm thick
approx. 600ml good quality olive oil
3 bay leaves
3 strips of pared lemon zest
2 large thyme sprigs
½ teaspoon black peppercorns

For the salad

1kg small waxy potatoes, such as Charlotte
1 large red pepper
2 continental salad onions, thinly sliced
2 tablespoons small capers, rinsed and drained, plus extra to garnish

For the dressing

6 tablespoons extra virgin olive oil
2 tablespoons lemon juice
sea salt and freshly ground black pepper

The day before you wish to serve this dish, make the tuna confit. Rub the tuna all over with 2 teaspoons sea salt and set aside for 1 hour. Put the oil, bay leaves, lemon zest, thyme and peppercorns into a pan in which the tuna will fit quite snugly and heat it to 60°C. Leave over a low heat, trying to maintain this temperature, for 20 minutes. Then remove and set aside.

Add the piece of salted tuna to the oil and bring the temperature of the oil up to 85°C. Leave at this temperature for 10 minutes, then remove from the heat and allow to cool, by which time the tuna should be perfectly cooked through. Transfer to a glass bowl or plastic box, cover and refrigerate until needed.

For the salad, cook the potatoes in well-salted water for 15–20 minutes until tender. Meanwhile, place the red pepper under a hot grill and cook for 20 minutes, turning it now and then, until the skin is quite black. Remove and drop into a plastic bag to cool, then remove and discard the stalk, seeds and skin and cut the flesh into thin strips.

Drain the potatoes and break them into small chunks into a bowl. For the dressing, whisk the olive oil and lemon juice together with ½ teaspoon sea salt and some black pepper. While the potatoes are still warm, stir in the dressing and leave them to cool. Then stir in the salad onions, capers and a little more seasoning to taste.

Remove the tuna from the oil and flake 150g of it into small chunks. Spoon the potato salad onto a shallow serving plate and scatter over the roasted red pepper strips and the flaked tuna. Scatter over a few more capers, drizzle with a little more oil and sprinkle with a little more sea salt, then serve.

Seared tuna steak with salsa verde on griddled potatoes

The last time I was cooking for my great friend and photographer Emma Lee, I overcooked the tuna – I was chatting too much and forgot to check it, but she was happy and satisfied when I cooked this dish for her for this book! Adding olives to a salsa verde gives extra flavour and an oiliness, which complements the tuna. This recipe makes a generous amount of salsa verde, but it is also wonderful served with grilled steaks.

Serves 4

500g small, evenly sized waxy potatoes, such as Charlotte

1 tablespoon olive oil, plus extra for brushing

4 x 200g tuna steaks, cut 3cm thick

sea salt and freshly ground black pepper

For the salsa verde

10g each of flat-leaf parsley leaves, mint leaves and basil leaves

1 garlic clove, thinly sliced

2 tablespoons salted capers, rinsed well, drained and dried

50g good-quality pitted green olives

4 anchovy fillets in oil

finely grated zest of ¼ small lemon

1 teaspoon Dijon mustard

1½ tablespoons lemon juice

8 tablespoons extra virgin olive oil

Cut the potatoes into 7–8mm-thick slices. Put them into a pan of well-salted cold water, bring to the boil and simmer for 5 minutes or until they are only just tender when pierced with the tip of a knife. Drain well, leave the steam to die down and then toss them with 1 tablespoon olive oil and some salt and pepper.

For the salsa verde, drop the herbs into boiling water, leave for 5 seconds, then drain and refresh under cold water. Squeeze out all the excess water, then put onto a chopping board with the sliced garlic, capers, olives and anchovies and finely chop everything together. Scoop the mixture into a bowl and stir in the lemon zest, mustard, lemon juice, olive oil and some freshly ground black pepper.

Heat a cast-iron griddle over a high heat, then lower the heat to medium. Add half the sliced potatoes in one layer and griddle for about 3 minutes on each side until golden. Transfer to a baking tray, sprinkle with a little more salt and keep hot in a low oven while you cook the remainder. Add them to the tray and keep hot.

Brush the tuna steaks with oil and season. Return the cast-iron griddle to a high heat and, when it is smoking hot, reduce the heat to medium-high. Place the steaks side-by-side on the griddle and cook for 1–1½ minutes on each side until nicely marked on the outside but still rare in the centre.

As you turn the tuna steaks over, divide the potatoes between 4 warmed plates. Put the tuna on top, spoon over some of the salsa verde and serve.

Salad of pears, mojama, rocket, pine nuts and olive oil

Mojama **is filleted salt-cured and air-dried tuna from Cadiz. Tuna loins are salted for 2 days, then the salt is removed and the tuna is laid out to dry in the sun for 15–20 days. Everyone knows the classic combination of pears, nuts and blue cheese – here the salty** *mojama* **works like the blue cheese to create a pleasing balance of tastes and textures.**

Serves 4

2 ripe but firm dessert pears

75g wild rocket

75g *mojama* (salt-cured and air-dried tuna), thinly shaved

40g pine nuts, toasted

For the dressing

3 tablespoons extra virgin olive oil

1 tablespoon lemon juice

2 teaspoons clear honey

1 teaspoon Dijon mustard

sea salt and freshly ground black pepper

To make the dressing, whisk together the olive oil, lemon juice, honey, mustard and some salt and pepper.

Quarter, core and peel the pears and then cut them lengthways into thin wedges. Put them into a bowl and toss them with 1 tablespoon of the dressing. Toss the rocket in another bowl with another tablespoon of the dressing.

Arrange the pears and rocket on 4 plates and drizzle over the remaining dressing. Scatter over the *mojama* shavings and pine nuts and serve.

Deep-fried red mullet with green olive mayonnaise and dressed green leaves

Every time I go to southern Spain I gorge on fried fish, and the red mullet from this area of the Mediterranean is exceptional. The Andalucians love to deep-fry fish, simply dusted in fine breadcrumbs and flour. If you want more crispiness, you can use gram flour. I like to put green olives in mayonnaise – I use the Andalucian Manzanilla olives, but if you can't get hold of them use good-quality, large, juicy, fresh green olives. This is my brother Antonio's, favourite recipe.

Serves 4

olive or sunflower oil, for deep-frying

4 x 225–275g whole red mullet, cleaned and trimmed

plain flour, for coating

sea salt and freshly ground black pepper

For the green olive mayonnaise

½ quantity Olive Oil Mayonnaise (see page 227)

1 teaspoon sherry vinegar

finely grated zest of ½ small lemon

1 tablespoon finely chopped shallot

2 teaspoons finely chopped green olives

2 teaspoons finely chopped cornichons

2 teaspoons capers, rinsed, drained and chopped

2 teaspoons chopped flat-leaf parsley

For the dressed green leaves

1 soft-leaved lettuce, broken into leaves

1 large continental salad onion, thinly sliced

3 tablespoons extra virgin olive oil

1 tablespoon lemon juice

pinch of caster sugar

Mix all the ingredients for the green olive mayonnaise with some salt to taste and spoon it into a small serving bowl.

Toss the lettuce leaves in a bowl with the salad onion. Make a dressing by whisking the extra virgin olive oil with the lemon juice, sugar and seasoning and set aside.

Heat some oil for deep-frying to 180°C (use a cooking thermometer) and preheat the oven to 110°C/gas mark ¼. Season the fish inside and out, coat generously with flour and shake off the excess. Deep-fry one at a time for 3 minutes until cooked through. Lift onto kitchen paper and keep hot in the oven while you cook the other fish.

Toss the lettuce leaves with the dressing and serve with the fried fish and the green olive mayonnaise.

Whole sea bass baked on anchovy and garlic potatoes

You can make this recipe with any whole large fish. Red snapper is especially good if you can't easily get hold of sea bass. This is a great celebratory dish for a special occasion – I love to make this for all my friends.

Serves 6

1.5kg large waxy potatoes, such as Desirée or Charlotte

4 large garlic cloves, thinly sliced

8 anchovy fillets in olive oil, drained and sliced

1 whole (approx. 1.75kg) sea bass or red snapper, cleaned and scaled

1 lemon, thinly sliced

3 bay leaves

3 lemon leaves (if available)

sea salt and freshly ground black pepper

For the dressing

8 tablespoons extra virgin olive oil

3 tablespoons lemon juice

3 tablespoons chopped oregano or marjoram

Preheat the oven to 200°C/gas mark 6. Make the dressing by whisking the olive oil with the lemon juice, 1½ teaspoons salt and some pepper, then stir in the chopped oregano or marjoram. Cut the potatoes into 8–10mm-thick slices and put them into a large roasting tin in which the fish fits either lengthways or diagonally. Add 6 tablespoons of the dressing, the sliced garlic and anchovies and toss well together. Spread out in an even layer and roast in the oven for 30–35 minutes.

Slash the flesh of the fish 5–6 times on each side. Season the cavity with salt and pepper, then stuff it with the lemon slices, bay leaves and lemon leaves (if using). Remove the tray of potatoes from the oven and release the slices from the bottom of the tin if they have stuck. Brush the outside of the fish with a little of the remaining dressing and season with salt and pepper. Put it on top of the potatoes and pour any remaining dressing into the cavity of the fish. Return the roasting tin to the oven and roast for a further 35 minutes until the fish is cooked through and the potatoes are tender. Serve hot.

Spicy lamb albondigas

It is believed that the concept of *albondigas* (meatballs) came from the Moors, with their dish of *kofte*. In Spain, lamb is not often used for meatballs, but I love the combination of lamb with these spices and ham. In my family, we always eat meatballs with *patatas fritas*, but you can serve them with plain rice. I presented this recipe on *Saturday Kitchen* and everyone loved it.

Serves 4

40g crustless white bread, thinly sliced

3 tablespoons milk

120g Serrano ham, thinly sliced

600g minced lamb

2 garlic cloves, crushed

1½ teaspoons freshly ground cumin seeds

1½ teaspoons freshly ground coriander seeds

¾ teaspoon hot *pimentón*

2 tablespoons chopped flat-leaf parsley

4 tablespoons olive oil, for frying

sea salt and freshly ground black pepper

For the sauce

3 tablespoons olive oil

150g shallots, finely chopped

3 garlic cloves, crushed

½ teaspoon crushed dried chillies

800g skinned, chopped vine-ripened tomatoes, fresh or canned

200ml good-quality Fino sherry

200ml homemade chicken stock

2 bay leaves

To serve

chopped flat-leaf parsley

extra virgin olive oil

1 quantity *patatas fritas* (see page 117)

Soak the bread in the milk for 5 minutes. Put the Serrano ham into a food processor and chop finely, using the pulse button. Squeeze the excess milk from the bread and put it into a bowl with the chopped ham, minced lamb, garlic, spices, parsley, ¼ teaspoon of salt and some pepper. Mix well together, then shape into about 32 meatballs (approx. 25g each).

Heat half the olive oil in a large frying pan over a medium-high heat. Add some of the meatballs and fry until golden brown all over. Remove them from the pan. Continue to fry the meatballs in batches, adding the remaining olive oil as necessary, until they are all browned.

For the sauce, heat the olive oil in a wide deep frying pan. Add the shallots, garlic and crushed dried chillies and fry gently for 8–10 minutes until soft but not browned. Add the tomatoes, sherry, stock, bay leaves and some salt and black pepper and simmer very gently, stirring now and then, for 1 hour until it has reduced and thickened.

Add the meatballs and simmer gently for 5 minutes or until heated through. Remove and discard the bay leaves. Spoon the meatballs onto a plate, scatter with a little chopped parsley and drizzle with a little extra virgin olive oil. Serve with *patatas fritas*.

Deep-fried chicken wings al ajillo

These chicken wings are great for a party and go really well with sherry – especially *Amontillado abocado.* **They are served in all the tapas bars in Andalusia. Normally you don't use too much chilli, but I love to add a real kick of heat to my** *ajillo* **(garlic dressing) – it must be the influence of living in London all these years!**

Serves 6

24 large, meaty, free-range chicken wings

olive or sunflower oil, for deep-frying

For the ajillo

6 fat garlic cloves

6 tablespoons extra virgin olive oil

1½ teaspoons crushed dried chillies

1½ teaspoons sweet *pimentón*

4 teaspoons sherry vinegar

sea salt

Cut off the pointy tips from each chicken wing and discard. Dry the wings well on kitchen paper. Heat the oil for deep-frying to 180°C (use a cooking thermometer). Add a quarter of the chicken wings and cook for 6–7 minutes until cooked through, crisp and golden.

Meanwhile, for the dressing, put the garlic cloves on a board, sprinkle with some salt and crush them into a smooth paste with the blade of a large knife. Put the extra virgin olive oil and the garlic in a small pan and place it over a medium-low heat. As soon as the garlic begins to sizzle, add the crushed dried chillies and cook very gently for about 2 minutes, until the garlic is very lightly golden. Stir in the *pimentón* and sherry vinegar and remove from the heat.

As soon as the first batch of chicken wings is cooked, drain them briefly on kitchen paper, tip them into a serving bowl and drizzle with some of the warm garlic and chilli dressing. Toss well together, sprinkle with a little sea salt and serve hot. Repeat with the remaining wings.

Pan-fried duck with a sherry, raisin and pine nut sauce

As Jerez is in the south of Spain, I have used sherry for this dish. In my cooking, I use Oloroso sherry in the same way as red wine, but Oloroso gives extra flavour because of the yeast in the sherry.

Serves 4

50g raisins

300ml Oloroso sherry

4 x 175–200g duck breasts

25g caster sugar

1 tablespoon red wine vinegar

¾ teaspoon arrowroot

2 teaspoons sherry vinegar

25g pine nuts, toasted

sea salt and freshly ground black pepper

watercress sprigs, to garnish

Soak the raisins in the sherry overnight. Remove the duck breasts from their packaging, put them on a plate, cover them loosely with a sheet of greaseproof paper and leave them somewhere cool overnight. This will help to dry out the skin and make it extra crispy.

The next day, put the sugar into a small pan with 1 tablespoon cold water and leave over a low heat until the sugar has completely dissolved. Increase the heat and boil vigorously until the syrup turns into a deep amber-coloured caramel. Remove the pan from the heat and add the vinegar (take care as it will bubble quite energetically). Return the pan to the heat, add the soaked raisins and the sherry and leave to simmer gently for 20 minutes. Mix the arrowroot with 2 tablespoons water, stir into the sauce and simmer for 1 minute. Season to taste and keep warm over a low heat.

Lightly score the skin of each duck breast into a diamond pattern, taking care not to cut down into the flesh. Season the meat with salt and pepper and the skin with just salt.

Heat a dry, heavy-based frying pan over a high heat. Add the duck breasts, skin-side down, lower the heat to medium and cook them for 3–4 minutes until the skin is crisp and golden brown. Turn the breasts over and cook them for 5 minutes if you like them pink, or slightly longer if you like them a little more cooked.

Remove the breasts from the pan onto a board and leave them to rest for 5 minutes. Then slice each one diagonally into long thin slices and transfer onto 4 warmed plates. Stir the sherry vinegar and toasted pine nuts into the sauce and spoon it over the duck. Garnish with the watercress and serve.

Oxtail with cinnamon, red wine, sherry vinegar and prunes

Oxtail are often eaten in southern Spain, and this is my adaption of the classical oxtail stews. When you cook the prunes with vinegar they caramelise to give a wonderful flavour.

Serves 4–6

2kg oxtail, cut into chunks

plain flour, for coating

5 tablespoons olive oil

5 tablespoons sherry vinegar

2 medium onions, chopped

1 small head of garlic, separated into cloves and peeled

5cm cinnamon stick

½ teaspoon ground allspice

200g skinned, chopped tomatoes, fresh or canned

500ml red wine, such as Tempranillo

500ml beef stock

4 strips of pared orange zest

1 bouquet garni (parsley stalks, bay leaves and thyme)

1–2 tablespoons clear honey

250g dried prunes (not the no-soak ones)

200ml port

400g small shallots or baby onions, peeled

300g carrots, cut into small chunks

2 celery sticks, sliced

sea salt and freshly ground black pepper

chopped parsley, to garnish

Olive Oil Mash or *patatas fritas*, to serve (see pages 33 and 117)

Season the oxtail well with salt and pepper, then coat the pieces in flour and knock off the excess. Heat 3 tablespoons of the oil in a large, flameproof casserole, add half the oxtail pieces and fry until well-browned all over. Do this slowly so that you get a really rich brown colour and lots of flavour without it burning on the base of the casserole. Lift the first batch into a bowl and repeat with the remainder.

Pour the excess oil from the casserole into a small bowl. Add the sherry vinegar to the pan and scrape the base with a wooden spoon as the liquid boils to release all the caramelised bits. Add to the bowl with the oxtail.

Return 3 tablespoons of the reserved oil to the casserole with the onions and garlic cloves, cover and cook, stirring now and then, for 10–12 minutes until soft and golden brown. Stir in the cinnamon, allspice and the tomatoes and fry for 2–3 minutes more. Add the red wine, beef stock, orange zest, bouquet garni and 1 tablespoon of the honey. Return the oxtail, all the juices from the bowl and some seasoning, bring to the boil, cover and simmer gently for 2½ hours, turning the pieces of oxtail over now and then, until just tender but not falling apart.

Remove the casserole from the heat and discard the cinnamon stick and herbs and leave to cool, then chill overnight. Put the prunes into a small bowl with the port and leave them to soak overnight.

The next day, remove the fat from the surface of the casserole and bring it back to a simmer over a low heat. Heat the remaining olive oil in a large pan. Add the shallots or baby onions, cover and fry gently until golden brown all over. Add the carrots and celery and fry for a further 5 minutes until lightly browned. Stir into the oxtail with the prunes and port. Re-cover and simmer for 30 minutes until the vegetables are tender. Stir in a little more honey if you wish and adjust the seasoning to taste. Sprinkle with the chopped parsley and serve with olive oil mash or *patatas fritas*.

Flamenquin

These are among one of the most popular tapa in Andalucia and the literal translation is 'small flamenco dancer'. They are fried veal, ham and cheese rolls.

Serves 4

4 x 150g veal or pork escalopes

8 thin slices of Serrano ham

100g *Queso de Grazalema* or Gruyère cheese, cut into 8 long sticks about 1cm thick

olive oil, for shallow-frying

plain flour, for coating

2 large free-range eggs, beaten

100g white breadcrumbs

For the tomato sauce

100ml olive oil

1 large onion, finely chopped

4 garlic cloves, finely chopped

400g skinned, chopped tomatoes, fresh or canned

150ml chicken stock

3 bay leaves

1 tablespoon chopped oregano or marjoram

2 tablespoons small capers, rinsed and drained

25g pitted black olives, cut lengthways into strips

Sugar, salt and freshly ground black pepper

For the tomato sauce, heat the olive oil in a medium pan. Add the onion and garlic, cover and cook gently for 10 minutes until very soft and lightly golden. Add the tomatoes, chicken stock and bay leaves and simmer, uncovered, for 30–40 minutes, stirring now and then, until the sauce has reduced and thickened to a good consistency.

Meanwhile, prepare the escalopes. Place each one in turn between 2 sheets of clingfilm and gently flatten with a rolling pin until uniformly thin. Cut each one in half and season lightly on both sides. Cover the pieces with a slice of Serrano ham. Lay the lengths of cheese across one short edge of each escalope, neatly roll them up and secure in place with a wooden cocktail stick.

Remove the bay leaves from the tomato sauce and discard, spoon half of it into a mini food processor and blend until smooth. Stir it back into the pan with the oregano or marjoram, capers, olives and some sugar, salt and pepper to taste and leave to simmer for a further 5 minutes. Keep hot.

Meanwhile, pour 2.5cm of olive oil in a deep sauté pan or wide-based saucepan and heat to 170°C (use a cooking thermometer). Dip the rolls first into the flour, then the beaten eggs and finally the breadcrumbs, and ensure they are well coated. Add them to the hot oil and fry for 5–7 minutes, turning them over frequently, until they are golden brown and cooked through. Drain briefly on kitchen paper, carefully remove the cocktail sticks and serve with the tomato sauce.

Hanging poached peaches with lemon and olive oil ice cream

In Spain they wrap the peaches in tissue paper when they are hanging on the tree, so I love the idea of 'hanging poached peaches'. You can make the peaches and keep them preserved in bottles. My mum used to do this so we could eat peaches throughout the year. For the ice cream, use the best fruity Arbequina olive oil that you can find – it is perfectly mild and fruity.

Serves 4

4 large, ripe peaches
1 vanilla pod
500ml sweet white wine, such as Moscatel de Chipiona
2 tablespoons clear honey

For the ice cream

200ml whole milk
5 large egg yolks
100g caster sugar
300ml double cream
finely grated zest of 1 lemon
150ml fruity Arbequina olive oil

For the ice cream, bring the milk to the boil in a medium pan. Meanwhile, whisk the egg yolks with the sugar until pale and thick. Gradually whisk in the hot milk, strain the mixture back into the pan and cook over a gentle heat, stirring constantly, until the mixture coats the back of a wooden spoon. Remove from the heat, leave to cool, then stir in the cream, lemon zest and olive oil and refrigerate overnight.

The next day, churn the ice-cream mixture in an ice-cream machine. Alternatively pour it into a shallow container and freeze until almost solid. Scrape into the bowl of a food processor and blend briefly until smooth, then return to the container and freeze once again. Repeat this 2–3 times more until the mixture is very smooth. Return to the freezer for 6 hours until firm or until needed.

Put the peaches into a heatproof bowl. Fill another bowl with iced water. Cover the peaches with boiling water and leave for 30 seconds, then remove and drop into the iced water. The skins should now peel away easily.

Slice the vanilla pod in half lengthways and scrape out the seeds with a tip of a knife. Put the pod and seeds into a pan (choose one in which the peaches will fit snugly in a single layer) with the sweet wine and honey and heat gently until the honey has dissolved. Add the peaches, bring to a simmer, cover and cook very gently for 15 minutes, carefully turning them over now and then with a wooden spoon, until they are just tender and can be pierced easily through to the stone with a cocktail stick.

When the peaches are cooked, gently transfer them and the vanilla pod to a bowl. Return the syrup to the heat and boil rapidly until reduced to 200ml. Leave to cool, then pour back over the peaches and chill until needed. Serve with the lemon and olive oil ice cream.

Flan de naranja

I remember coming home when I was a child and going to the fridge, taking out a whole flan (crème caramel) and eating it all. In Spain we make one large flan rather than small individual ones. I think this dish is even better with the addition of orange zest; it is now top of my list of desserts and that's why I serve it in my restaurant Pizarro.

Serves 8–10

175g caster sugar, plus 75g

1 litre whole milk

finely grated zest of 8 large oranges

6 large free-range eggs, plus 6 large free-range egg yolks

Preheat the oven to 170°C/gas mark 3. Place a shallow 1.5-litre oval baking dish into the oven to warm. Put 175g of the sugar into a medium pan with 100ml cold water and leave it over a low heat until the sugar has dissolved, then increase the heat and boil rapidly until the mixture has turned into a dark amber caramel. Remove from the heat and quickly pour the caramel into the warmed dish, tilting it backwards and forwards to cover the base and 1cm up the sides in a thin, even layer. Set aside.

Put the milk, remaining sugar and orange zest into a clean pan and bring to simmering point. Remove from the heat and set aside for 30 minutes.

Put the eggs and egg yolks into a bowl and whisk together lightly. Strain the orange-infused milk and whisk it into the eggs. Pour the mixture into the baking dish and put it into a small roasting tin. Pour hot (but not boiling) water into the tin until it comes halfway up the sides of the dish. Bake in the oven for 45–50 minutes or until the mixture has just set but still has a slight wobble in the centre. It will continue to firm up as it cools. Remove the dish from the roasting tin and leave to cool, then chill for 6 hours or overnight.

To serve, run a round-bladed knife around the edge of the dish and invert onto a serving dish. Pour over the caramel juices and serve.

Strawberries in sherry vinegar with goat's cheese parfait and praline

People often serve strawberries with balsamic vinegar, but sherry vinegar works just as well. The goat's cheese parfait adds a creaminess and the praline a sweet crunchiness.

Serves 8

500g small strawberries

4 teaspoons caster sugar

1 tablespoon sweet Pedro Ximenez sherry vinegar

For the goat's cheese parfait

200ml whole milk

5 large egg yolks

50g caster sugar

100ml double cream

150g soft, rindless goat's cheese

50g liquid glucose

100g whole-milk natural yogurt

For the praline

50g caster sugar

25g flaked almonds, toasted

For the goat's cheese parfait, bring the milk slowly to the boil in a medium non-stick pan. Meanwhile, beat together the egg yolks and sugar in a mixing bowl until pale and creamy. Whisk the hot milk into the egg yolks, return the mixture to the pan and stir over a low heat until the mixture thickens and coats the back of a wooden spoon. Pour into a bowl and leave to cool. Stir in the cream and chill overnight.

The next day, put the goat's cheese into a bowl with the liquid glucose and yogurt and beat until smooth, then gradually beat in the chilled custard. Churn the mixture in an ice-cream machine. Alternatively pour it into a shallow container and freeze until almost solid. Scrape into the bowl of a food processor and blend briefly until smooth, then return to the container and freeze once again. Repeat this 2–3 times more until the mixture is very smooth. Spoon the mixture evenly into 8 dariole moulds or small ramekins of 120ml capacity, cover with clingfilm and freeze for 4 hours until firm or until needed.

For the praline, line a baking tray with non-stick baking parchment. Put the caster sugar in a small pan with 2 tablespoons water. Leave over a low heat until the sugar has completely dissolved, then boil rapidly until it has turned into a brick-red caramel. Remove from the heat, quickly stir in the flaked almonds, pour onto the paper-lined tray and spread out into a thin layer. Allow to become cold, then transfer to a mini food processor and blend briefly until finely crushed.

Shortly before serving, halve the strawberries into a bowl and stir in the sugar and sherry vinegar. Leave to stand for 5 minutes. Unmould the goat's cheese parfaits onto plates and sprinkle with praline. Spoon some of the strawberries alongside and serve.

You can store any leftover praline in an airtight container – it's lovely sprinkled over vanilla ice cream.

Candied orange torrijas with bitter orange caramel

Torrijas **is the Spanish form of British eggy bread or French** *pain perdue* **– fresh bread, soaked in a rich and creamy egg custard and then pan-fried in butter until crisp and golden. The twist of sweet candied orange and bitter orange caramel takes this to a more sophisticated level.**

Serves 4

For the torrijas

16 small, medium-thick slices of white bread

175g butter, softened

100g good-quality chopped candied
    orange peel

3 medium free-range eggs

120ml double cream, plus extra to serve

120ml whole milk

few drops of vanilla extract

50g caster sugar, for sprinkling

For the bitter orange caramel

75g caster sugar

2 tablespoons cold water

1 tablespoon orange liqueur

2½ tablespoons freshly squeezed orange
    juice, strained

For the bitter orange caramel, put the sugar and water into a small pan and leave over a low heat until the sugar has completely dissolved. Then increase the heat and leave the syrup to boil rapidly until it has turned into a brick-red caramel. Stand back and add the orange liqueur (it will splutter quite ferociously) and then plunge the base of the pan into cold water to stop it cooking any further. Return the pan to a low heat, add the orange juice and leave until all the caramel has dissolved once more. Tip the mixture into a bowl or small glass jar and leave to go cold. This can be made ahead of time if you wish.

For the *torrijas*, cut a 7cm disc from each slice of bread and spread with a little of the butter. Spoon the candied mixed peel into the buttered centre of 8 of the discs, cover with the remaining 8 discs, buttered side down, and press well together around the edges to seal.

Beat together the eggs, cream, milk and vanilla extract in a shallow dish. Gently melt the remaining butter in a small pan and pour off the clear butter into a small bowl, leaving behind the milky-white liquid at the bottom of the pan.

Pour some of the clarified butter into a large non-stick frying pan and place it over a medium heat. Dip the *torrijas* into the egg mixture one at a time, leave for a few seconds, then turn over, making sure they are evenly coated and well soaked in the mixture. Add some of them to the frying pan and fry for 2 minutes on each side until crisp and golden. Drain briefly on kitchen paper and keep hot. Repeat with the remaining butter and *torrijas*. Serve hot, sprinkled with caster sugar and drizzled with a little double cream and some of the bitter orange caramel.

Almond, raisin and lemon cake

This is a deliciously moist cake studded with raisins. The recipe was inspired by the exceptional Malaga raisins of the region. It can be served warm as a dessert or is excellent cold with strong coffee. It keeps well for a few days in an airtight tin.

Serves 10–12

175g softened butter, plus extra for greasing

60g plain flour, plus extra for dusting

75g good-quality raisins

215g caster sugar, plus extra for dusting

finely grated zest of 1 lemon

4 large free-range eggs

115g ground almonds

2 tablespoons lemon juice

Preheat the oven to 180°C/gas mark 4. Grease a 20cm loose-based cake tin with sides 5cm deep and base-line with non-stick baking parchment. Grease the paper and then dust the tin with a little flour. Put the raisins into a food processor with 2 teaspoons of the flour and whizz briefly using the pulse button until they are finely chopped. Beat the butter and sugar together in a mixing bowl until very pale and fluffy. Add the lemon zest. Beat in the eggs, one at a time, adding a little of the flour with the last egg. Fold in the remaining flour, the ground almonds, raisins and lemon juice. Spoon the mixture evenly into the prepared tin and bake for 45 minutes, loosely covering the top with a sheet of foil after 30 minutes to stop it browning too much. Run a knife around the outside of the cake and turn it out onto a cooling rack covered with a sheet of kitchen paper. Remove the base of the tin and the lining paper, cover with a second cooling rack and turn it back over again. Dust with caster sugar and leave to cool.

Payoyo with Seville orange chutney

Payoyo is a very rich, hard sheep's cheese from Cadiz, from the beautiful area of Grazalema. If you can't get it, use a well-known Manchego. Seville oranges are normally used to make marmalade, but this chutney is stunning and goes so well with this local cheese.

Serves 8

500g Payoyo cheese, thinly sliced

For the Seville orange chutney

50g raisins

4 tablespoons sherry vinegar

4 tablespoons Oloroso sherry

25g butter

1 tablespoon olive oil

250g pickling onions (or small shallots), peeled

50g shallots, finely chopped

juice of 3 Seville oranges (about 9 tablespoons) or 6 tablespoons orange juice and 3 tablespoons lemon juice

5 tablespoons coarse-cut Seville orange marmalade

8 cloves

pinch of ground allspice

fine sea salt

Put the raisins, sherry vinegar and sherry into a small pan and bring to a simmer over a low heat. Remove from the heat and leave the raisins to plump up for 30 minutes.

Heat the butter and olive oil in a medium pan, add the pickling onions, cover and cook gently for 10 minutes, shaking the pan now and then, until they are golden brown and starting to soften.

Stir in the chopped shallots, re-cover and cook gently for 5 minutes until soft. Add the raisin and sherry vinegar mixture, re-cover the pan and continue to cook gently for 10 minutes until the pickling onions are now quite soft. Add the Seville orange (or orange and lemon) juice, the marmalade, cloves, allspice and a good pinch of salt, part-cover the pan and simmer, stirring occasionally, for 20 minutes or until the onions have just collapsed and the mixture has reduced and thickened. Allow to cool and then serve with thin slices of Payoyo cheese.

THE ISLANDS

THE ISLANDS: INTRODUCTION

The Canary and the Balearic islands are much more than tourist destinations with big hotels and all-day and all-night clubs. Away from the hot spots there are also incredible areas of tranquillity and amazing beaches. And the great gastronomic culture of these islands is protected by the water that surrounds them. Even though they are hundreds of miles apart, the food of these two sets of islands are similar in their simplicity, freshness and strong flavours.

I have to admit that my first visit to the Canaries was for the Carnival of Tenerife, which is one of the things that you have to do once in your life, when you are young! The carnival spirit was imported for sure, from the New World, since the ports of the Canary Islands were very important stopping places during the age of sea-faring discoverers and conquerors. The links are evident from the islanders' colourful cultural dress as well as from the diversity of tropical fruits that are now cultivated here: mangoes, avocados, pineapples and bananas. I can still recall the incredible contrast of the thronging beach resorts and high-rise hotels with the jungle-like banana plantations that are so huge you could easily become lost.

The Canary Islands are not just known for their tropical fruits, but for the great variety of stews – my favourite is the Canary stew (on page 197), the *mojos* or cold sauces made with a base of oil and vinegar and served as a dressing to accompany fish or meat, and one of the islands' star dishes: 'wrinkled potatoes' – *patatas arrugas* (page 191), which have become a must-have snack at almost all of my parties at home.

My earliest gastronomic memory of the Balearic Islands is from Menorca, the most easterly of the group. It was a delicious lobster stew, *caldereta de langosta* – a speciality of the island, which encapsulates the healthy, simple style of Mediterranean cuisine. As the locals will tell you, lobsters from the warm shallow waters around Menorca have an exquisitely delicate and sweet flavour. One of Spain's few cheeses made from cow's milk is made on Menorca, called Mahón. It is slightly sharp, with a salty tang and it's one of my favourite cheeses.

Pork is a very important ingredient in Balearic cuisine. For me the most notable speciality is the *sobrasada*, a soft, spicy sausage that I love to eat with toast and a drizzle of honey. On Majorca you will often see people returning home with a round box that contains an *ensaïmada*, which is a type of yeast-based pastry made with pork lard, which is fashioned into a coil before being baked. You must try both of these things if you are lucky enough to be in the Balearics.

As a Spaniard, the whole world wants to know about my holiday experiences in Ibiza, and it comes as a surprise to learn that I have never been to the 'party capital of the world'. To tell the truth, I would sooner relax on one of the beautiful beaches and stay in an agroturismo, a small rural house, and enjoy the countryside and local cuisine. I am getting old! The landscape and local food of all the Balearic Islands are just too good to be missed.

Avocado with prawns and tomato vinaigrette

When I was a child, it was very rare to find avocados on the Spanish mainland, but you did see them on the islands. Of course, they are now found all over Spain and there are big growers in Andalusia. For this recipe, I marry avocados with prawns for a classic combination, but please try the tomato vinaigrette with it. The buttery flavour of the avocados, sweetness from the prawns and the acidity of the tomatoes make this dish a perfect summer starter.

Serves 4

2 ripe but firm avocados

20 cooked large prawns or crevettes, peeled

1 roasted red pepper, skinned, deseeded and cut into long thin strips

1 fat continental salad onion or 3 spring onions, thinly sliced

1 teaspoon chopped flat-leaf parsley

For the tomato vinaigrette

250g vine-ripened tomatoes, skinned and deseeded

1 small garlic clove, crushed to a paste with a little salt

2 tablespoons red wine vinegar

¼ teaspoon caster sugar

2–3 tablespoons extra virgin olive oil, plus extra to serve (depending on the juiciness of the tomatoes)

sea salt and freshly ground black pepper

For the tomato vinaigrette, put the tomato flesh into a mini food processor with the garlic, vinegar, sugar, ½ teaspoon salt and some pepper and blend everything together until smooth. With the motor still running, gradually add the olive oil.

Cut each of the avocados in half and remove and discard the stones. Peel off the skin, place cut-side down onto a board and cut the flesh across on the diagonal into thin slices.

Spoon 2 tablespoons of the tomato vinaigrette into the centre of 4 small plates. Arrange the avocado slices and peeled prawns on top. Arrange the red pepper strips in amongst them and then spoon over a further 2 tablespoons of the dressing. Sprinkle over the onion and chopped parsley, drizzle with a little more oil and serve with some fresh crusty bread.

Salt-crusted potatoes with coriander mojo

Everyone thinks that coriander came from the Americas to Spain because it is eaten there in great quantities, but, believe it or not the herb was taken there by the *conquistadores*. Coriander is very popular in the Canary Islands and this *mojo* (sauce) is found everywhere there. This dish of *patatas arrugas* ('wrinkled potatoes') is a perfect tapa for a party and very healthy because of all the garlic! You can always cut down the amount of garlic if you prefer. Jersey Royals are my favourite potato, but use any type of new potato if they are out of season.

Serves 6

1kg evenly sized Jersey Royal potatoes, scrubbed but unpeeled

sea salt flakes

For the coriander mojo

3 large garlic cloves, roughly chopped

1 green chilli, deseeded and chopped

leaves from a 20g bunch of coriander, roughly chopped

1 teaspoon freshly ground cumin seeds

100ml extra virgin olive oil

2 teaspoons white wine vinegar, Moscatel if possible

Put the potatoes into a wide shallow pan in which they fit in a single layer. Add 30g salt and 1 litre cold water (enough just to cover), bring to the boil and leave to boil rapidly until the water has evaporated. Then turn the heat to low and continue to cook for a few minutes, gently turning the potatoes over now and again, until they are dry and the skins are wrinkled and covered in a thin crust of salt.

While the potatoes are cooking, make the coriander *mojo*. Put the garlic, green chilli and 1 teaspoon salt in a mortar and pound into a paste. Add the coriander leaves and pound until they are incorporated into the paste. Add the cumin and gradually mix in the oil to make a smooth sauce. Just before serving, stir in the vinegar and spoon into a small bowl.

Pile the hot potatoes onto a plate and serve with the *mojo*, instructing your guests to rub off as much salt from the potatoes as they wish before dipping them into the sauce.

Roasted squash with dried chilli, honey, cinnamon and pine nuts

This can be a side dish for any grilled fish or meat. I serve it with Ibérico pork cheeks or any game stew. It is also delicious on its own.

Serves 4–6

1.5kg unprepared squash (butternut, onion
   or kabocha)

4 tablespoons olive oil

1 fat garlic clove, finely chopped

½ teaspoon crushed dried chillies

½ teaspoon ground cinnamon

25g pine nuts

50ml clear honey

sea salt flakes and freshly ground
   black pepper

Preheat the oven to 200°C/gas mark 6. Halve the squash through the stem end, scoop out the seeds, peel and then cut into 2.5–3cm-thick wedges.

Put the oil into a roasting tin with the garlic, crushed dried chillies, cinnamon, 1 teaspoon sea salt flakes and plenty of freshly ground black pepper. Mix well together. Add the wedges of squash to the tin and turn them over a few times in the oil mixture until well coated. Sit them on their curved edges and roast them in the oven for 20 minutes.

Spread the pine nuts onto a baking tray and roast them in the oven alongside the squash for 5–6 minutes, giving them a stir now and then, until they are all golden. Remove and set aside.

Remove the squash from the oven and brush the wedges with some of the honey. Return to the oven and roast for a further 15 minutes, brushing with more of the honey and then the caramelised juices, every 5 minutes, until the squash is tender and slightly caramelised. Brush one last time with the juices from the pan, pile onto a serving plate and scatter over the pine nuts.

Scrambled eggs with tomatoes, Serrano ham and avocado

You might think it's a bit crazy to have scrambled egg with avocado but, with its Latin American influence, this recipe works well and is delicious served with tortillas.

Serves 4

3 tablespoons olive oil

1 small onion, finely chopped

1 large garlic clove, finely chopped

1 green chilli, finely chopped

350g vine-ripened tomatoes, skinned, deseeded and diced

75g Serrano ham, finely chopped

2–3 tablespoons chopped coriander, plus extra to garnish

8 large free-range eggs, beaten

1 small ripe but firm avocado, stoned, peeled and cut into small dice

warm flour tortillas (see page 229), to serve

sea salt and freshly ground black pepper

Heat the olive oil in a medium, deep-sided, non-stick frying pan over a medium heat. Add the onion, garlic, chilli and some seasoning, cover and cook gently for 10 minutes until soft. Stir in the tomatoes, cook for 5 minutes, then stir in the ham and cook for a further 1 minute.

Stir in the chopped coriander, followed by the beaten eggs and diced avocado, and stir over a medium-low heat until the eggs are softly scrambled. Spoon onto warmed plates, sprinkle with a little more chopped coriander and serve with the warm flour tortillas.

Russian-style sweetcorn salad with lobster and homemade crisps

I know you will wonder why there is a Russian salad in a Spanish book, but you will find the *ensaladilla Rusa* in restaurants and tapas bars all over Spain, with thousands of variations. It should be called a Spanish summer salad! In the Canaries they add in some sweetcorn as well. When I told my friend about this dish he thought I was mad, but I promise it is delicious! Ideally, you need a deep-fat fryer for the crisps.

Serves 6–8

2 x 450g cooked lobsters

1 large fresh sweetcorn cob or 175g fresh
  sweetcorn kernels

350g waxy potatoes

175g carrots, halved

100g fine green beans

50g petits pois, freshly shelled or frozen

½ quantity Olive Oil Mayonnaise
  (see page 227)

1½ teaspoons lemon juice

5 spring onions, thinly sliced

50g cornichons or gherkins, finely chopped

1 tablespoon chopped flat-leaf parsley

sea salt

For the homemade crisps

600g small, floury maincrop potatoes, such as
  King Edward

olive or groundnut oil, for deep-frying

First remove the meat from the lobsters. Twist off the claw arms and break each one into 3 pieces at the joints. Crack the shells of each claw with a large sharp knife and remove the meat. Slice open the meat from the largest claw, remove the very thin, flat piece of bone from the centre and discard. Remove the meat from the other pieces by hooking them out with a lobster pick. Try to keep the pieces of meat as large as possible. Pull the tail away from the head and discard the head. Place the tail belly-side down on a chopping board and, using a large, sharp knife, cut it in half lengthways. Separate the two halves and remove and discard the dark intestinal tract that runs along the top edge of the tail meat (there might be a little on each half). Lift out the piece of tail meat from each half and cut it across into thin slices. Put the meat onto a plate, cover and chill until you are ready to serve.

For the salad, stand the whole sweetcorn cob upright on a board and cut the kernels away, keeping the blade as close to the cob as you can. Cook the vegetables separately in boiling well-salted water until tender, then refresh them in a bowl of iced water. The potatoes will take about 12–15 minutes, the carrots about 8 minutes, the green beans 4 minutes, the sweetcorn 3 minutes and the peas 1 minute. Drain everything well, cut the potatoes into 1cm dice and the carrots and beans into similar-sized pieces.

Mix the mayonnaise with the lemon juice in a mixing bowl and then fold in the cooked vegetables, spring onions, chopped cornichons, parsley and some seasoning to taste.

For the crisps, peel the potatoes and slice them across, very thinly, ideally using a mandolin. Wash them in plenty of cold water to remove the starch and dry well – spin them first in a salad spinner, then dry them extra well on clean tea towels. Heat some oil for deep-frying to 180°C. Place a chip basket in the oil, drop in a large handful of the potato slices and fry for 1½–2 minutes, stirring them around every now and then, until golden brown and very crisp. Remove using the chip basket, shake off the excess oil and then spread the crisps over a paper-lined baking tray and leave to cool. Sprinkle with a little fine sea salt and set aside.

Spoon some of the salad onto 4 plates and arrange the lobster meat alongside. Pile some of the crisps onto the plate and serve.

Puchero Canario

**This is a *cocido*-like stew, served all
over the Canaries, but quite different
from all others in Spain because it uses
vegetables from the New World. It is so
popular that you can buy the necessary
meat and vegetables pre-packaged in
many of the supermarkets. I have simplified
the traditional recipe, keeping the key
flavours, but making it into more of a
chunky stew, which I sometimes serve with
a spoonful of the spicy red *mojo* (page 212).**

Serves 8

3 tablespoons olive oil

300g piece of unsmoked gammon, cut into
1cm-wide strips

4 x 100g chorizo sausages, skinned and each
cut into 6 chunky pieces

700g boneless chicken thigh fillets, cut in half

1 teaspoon crushed dried chillies

1 large onion, chopped

6 fat garlic cloves, thinly sliced

1 large carrot, cut into small chunks

2 teaspoons freshly ground cumin seeds

1 teaspoon saffron strands, lightly toasted,
then ground

400g cooked chickpeas

450g squash, such as kabocha or butternut,
peeled and cut into small chunky pieces

400g sweet potatoes, peeled and cut into
small chunky pieces

350g small waxy potatoes, such as Charlotte,
peeled and thickly sliced

2 fresh sweetcorn cobs, cut across into
1cm-thick slices

225g fine green beans, cut into 5cm pieces

200g courgettes, cut into 2cm dice

350g piece of spring cabbage, cut into
2.5cm-wide strips

sea salt and freshly ground black pepper

Heat the oil in a large flameproof casserole. Add the gammon strips and chorizo sausage and fry for 2 minutes until lightly golden. Remove with a slotted spoon onto a plate and set aside. Season the chicken pieces with salt and pepper, add to the casserole and fry until lightly golden on both sides. Remove and set aside with the gammon and chorizo.

Add the chilli flakes to the oil left in the pan and, as soon as they start to sizzle, add the onion, garlic and carrot, cover and fry gently for 5 minutes until the onion is soft.

Stir in the cumin and saffron and fry for 2 minutes, then add 1 litre water and bring to the boil. Stir in the chicken, chorizo, gammon and 1 teaspoon salt, cover and simmer for 15 minutes.

Uncover and stir in the chickpeas, squash, sweet and waxy potatoes and a little more salt if necessary, re-cover and simmer for 15 minutes. Uncover, add the sweetcorn pieces and green beans and simmer for 5 minutes, then stir in the courgettes and cabbage and simmer for a further 5 minutes, by which time all the vegetables should be tender. Adjust the seasoning to taste and serve.

Grilled mackerel with tomato, chilli and mint salad

I often combine oily fish with tomatoes to cut through the richness of the fish. It's the perfect combination. The chilli and mint add an extra kick to this beautiful summer salad.

Serves 4

1 garlic clove

1 teaspoon dried oregano

½ teaspoon sweet *pimentón*

2 tablespoons olive oil, plus extra for oiling

4 x 350g mackerel, cleaned, gutted and trimmed of their fins

sea salt and freshly ground black pepper

For the tomato, chilli and mint salad

600g ripe beef tomatoes, skinned

1 medium-hot red chilli, deseeded and finely chopped

1 large continental salad onion, thinly sliced

1 tablespoon red wine vinegar

3 tablespoons extra virgin olive oil

small bunch of mint leaves

75g small watercress sprigs

Preheat the grill to high. Crush the clove of garlic on a board under the blade of a large knife, sprinkle with a little salt and then work it into a paste with the blade. Put the paste into a bowl and mix in the dried oregano, *pimentón* and oil. Slash the mackerel on the diagonal at 8mm intervals along both sides and brush some of the *pimentón* oil inside the cavity as well as over the skin. Season inside and out and lay on an oiled baking tray or the rack of the grill pan.

For the tomato salad, halve the tomatoes and remove the seeds. Cut the flesh into small chunky pieces and scatter them over the base of a large serving plate. Sprinkle with some salt and pepper and then the chilli and salad onion. Whisk the vinegar and oil together with a little more seasoning and drizzle over the salad, then scatter over the mint, followed by the watercress sprigs. Grill the mackerel for 4–5 minutes on each side until cooked through. Serve with the salad.

Barbecued sardines with mango, red onion and coriander salsa

For me, you cannot beat sardines fresh from the sea, cooked on the barbecue and served with some thinly sliced red onion, dressed with a good olive oil and some sherry vinegar to help cut through the oiliness of the fish. The zingy salad adds another layer of flavour, which results in a really well-balanced dish.

Serves 6

12–16 fresh sardines

For the salsa

1 large ripe but firm mango

1 medium-hot red chilli, deseeded and finely chopped

½ small red onion, finely chopped

finely grated zest of ½ lime

2 teaspoons lime juice

20g coriander leaves, finely chopped

sea salt and freshly ground black pepper

To prepare the sardines, rub the scales off each fish with your thumb, working under running cold water, then gut them and trim off their fins.

If you are using a charcoal barbecue, light it 30 minutes or so before you want to start cooking. When it is ready to cook on, the coals should be covered in a layer of light grey ash. If using a gas barbecue, light it 10 minutes beforehand.

For the salsa, peel the mango and then slice the flesh away from either side of the flat stone in one piece and cut into small dice. Mix in a bowl with the remaining ingredients and set aside.

Barbecue the sardines for 2–3 minutes on each side until the skins blister and char a little and they are just cooked through. Serve with the salsa.

Pan-fried sardines with tomato and rosemary salsa templada

When I was child, we ate sardines at least once a week – fried, *a la plancha* (grilled on the barbecue), even straight from the basket raw. I love sardines so much. This warm dressing (*templada*) on sardines is my latest addition to the menu at Pizarro, my restaurant.

Serves 4

12 fresh sardines
4 tablespoons olive oil
sea salt and freshly ground black pepper
1 quantity Olive Oil Mash (see page 33), to serve

For the warm tomato dressing

1 small onion, finely chopped
1 garlic clove, finely chopped
1 tablespoon olive oil
250g skinned, deseeded and chopped tomatoes, fresh or canned
4 tablespoon red wine vinegar
1 teaspoon caster sugar
100ml extra virgin olive oil
1 tablespoon finely chopped rosemary

To prepare the sardines, rub the scales off each fish with your thumb, working under running cold water, then gut them and trim off the fins. Season them inside and out.

For the tomato dressing, gently fry the onion and garlic in the olive oil until soft but not browned. Add the tomatoes and simmer for 10–15 minutes. Meanwhile, put half the red wine vinegar and the sugar into a very small pan and boil rapidly until reduced to 1 teaspoon. Stir this into the tomato sauce, season well, then liquidise until smooth. Return to a clean pan and simmer if necessary until thick enough to coat the back of a wooden spoon. Keep warm. Put the rest of the vinegar into a small saucepan with the extra virgin olive oil, chopped rosemary and some seasoning and whisk well together. Set aside.

To cook the sardines, heat half the olive oil in a large frying pan, add half the fish and pan-fry for 3 minutes on each side until cooked through and lightly golden. Lift onto a baking tray and keep warm while you cook the remainder.

Stir the warm tomato sauce into the herb vinaigrette. Spoon some of the olive oil mash slightly to one side of each of 4 warmed plates and rest the sardines alongside. Spoon some of the dressing around the edge of the plate and serve.

Sautéed squid, onions and potatoes with chilli and sherry vinegar

This recipe is amazing. I love *calamari à la romana* (deep-fried squid), one of the most popular tapas all over Spain and synonymous with Spanish cooking, but I think calamari deserve more than that. This is one great example. The most important thing is to caramelise the onions well, so take your time.

Serves 4

5 tablespoons extra virgin olive oil

1 medium onion, halved and thinly sliced

250g small waxy potatoes, such as Charlotte, unpeeled

500g medium squid, cleaned

½ teaspoon crushed dried chillies

1 garlic clove, finely chopped

leaves from 2 large thyme sprigs

1 tablespoon sherry vinegar

1 tablespoon chopped flat-leaf parsley

sea salt and freshly ground black pepper

Heat 2 tablespoons of the oil in a large frying pan, add the onion, cover and cook over a low-medium heat, stirring now and then, for about 15 minutes until it is soft and nicely caramelised. Meanwhile, cook the potatoes in well-salted boiling water for 15 minutes until tender. Drain, peel and cut in half lengthways.

Slice the squid pouches across into 7–8mm-thick rings. Leave the tentacles as they are.

Heat another tablespoon of the oil in another small frying pan and add the potatoes cut-side down. Fry gently for 2–3 minutes, turning them over half way through, until crisp and nicely golden. Set aside over a very low heat.

Heat another tablespoon of the oil in a large frying pan, add half the squid and half the crushed dried chillies, season with salt and fry over a high heat for 1½ minutes, adding half the garlic halfway through, until the squid is cooked and nicely caramelised. Tip into the small frying pan with the potatoes to keep warm and fry the rest of the squid as before with the remaining oil, chilli and garlic. Return the first batch of squid, along with the potatoes, to the large pan, sprinkle in the thyme leaves and toss together briefly over a medium-high heat to mix them together. Drizzle in the sherry vinegar, add the chopped parsley, toss together once more and serve.

Sautéed squid with green beans and toasted almonds

This recipe is all about how to cook your squid perfectly. They must be cooked very quickly, as here, or really slowly – never in between. People don't often put nuts and fish together, but I think the nuttiness of the almonds works well with the squid and adds texture. I developed this recipe with my friend Esperanza and when we tried it, it went straight onto the menu. Even now, in José, I make it with runner beans *a la plancha*, but this dish is definitely the winner (because *a la plancha* means that the juices run out, whereas here you contain the caramelised juices from the squid).

Serves 4

250g fine green beans
500g medium squid, cleaned
2 tablespoons olive oil
2 garlic cloves, finely chopped
1 medium-hot red chilli, deseeded and finely chopped
1 tablespoon sherry vinegar
leaves from 2 large thyme sprigs, plus extra to garnish
30g flaked almonds, toasted, plus extra to garnish
sea salt and freshly ground black pepper

Bring a pan of well-salted water to the boil. Top and tail the green beans and cut them in half if very long. Drop them into the boiling water and cook for 3 minutes. Drain, refresh under cold water and drain well once more. Set aside.

Slit open the squid pouches along one side and cut in half lengthways, then cut each piece across into wide strips. Cut each bunch of tentacles in half. Put half the olive oil and half the garlic into a large frying pan and, as soon as the garlic starts to colour, add half the squid, half the chilli and some seasoning and stir-fry over a high heat for 2–3 minutes until the squid is just cooked through and lightly caramelised. Tip onto a plate and repeat with the remaining garlic, squid and chilli, but leave everything in the pan.

Return the first batch of squid and the green beans to the pan with the vinegar and cook briefly over a high heat for a few seconds. Add the thyme leaves and toasted flaked almonds and toss well together. Transfer onto a warmed serving plate, scatter with thyme leaves and flaked almonds and serve.

Lobster with warm lentil salad and romesco sauce

It is quite unusual to see lentils with shellfish; normally lentils are matched with game or meat (see pages 122 and 132). I wanted to try my lobster with romesco sauce and I was looking for more flavour to bring to the dish and found that the meaty, rich flavour of the lobster went well with the earthy lentils.

Serves 4

4 medium (approx. 450–500g) live lobsters

1 quantity Romesco Sauce (see page 228)

For the warm lentil salad

200g green lentils, such as pardina or Puy

2 tablespoons olive oil

2 garlic cloves, finely chopped

leaves from 2 large thyme sprigs,
    plus extra to garnish

1 tablespoon sweet Pedro Ximenez sherry
    vinegar or balsamic vinegar

sea salt and freshly ground black pepper

Put the live lobsters in the freezer for 1 hour to send them to sleep before cooking.

Check over the lentils for any small stones, then tip into a pan and cover by 5cm with cold water. Bring to the boil, lower the heat and leave to simmer for 30 minutes or until just cooked, adding a little salt to the pan 5 minutes before the end of cooking. Drain well.

Meanwhile, bring one or two large pans of water to the boil, adding 30g salt per litre of water. Add the lobsters, bring the water back to the boil and cook for 5 minutes. Remove them from the pan(s) and leave until cool enough to handle. Discard the water.

To remove the meat from the shell, break off the claws, break them open at each joint and remove the meat from each segment in pieces as large as possible. Break the tails away from the heads, which you can discard. Turn the tail upside down and, holding it in one hand, cut along either side of the flat belly shell with strong scissors. Pull back the flap of shell and lift out the tail meat. Repeat for each tail.

To finish the lentils, put 1 tablespoon of olive oil and garlic in a medium pan and place it over a medium heat. As soon as the garlic starts to sizzle add the thyme leaves and cook gently for 1 minute. Stir in the lentils and heat through gently. Stir in the vinegar and some seasoning to taste and keep warm over a low heat.

To finish the lobster, heat the remaining olive oil in a large non-stick frying pan over a medium heat. Add the lobster tails and sauté them gently for 2 minutes, turning now and then, until heated through. Add the claw meat 1 minute before they are ready.

Lift the lobster tails onto a board and slice each one across into 1cm-thick slices. Overlap the slices on 4 warmed plates and arrange the claw meat between the slices. Spoon the lentils next to the lobster and some of the romesco sauce alongside. Garnish with thyme sprigs and serve.

Lobster caldereta

This is a classic dish from the Balearic Islands where lobster is plentiful. This stew, or *caldereta*, is intensely flavoured with garlic and tomatoes, thickened with a paste of garlic, olive oil, parsley and the tomalley (the lobster liver) at the end. I like to serve the stew on toasted slices of bread spread with a little allioli (garlic mayonnaise), but it is just as good served on toasted bread rubbed with garlic and drizzled with olive oil. Or you can just serve it with some fresh crusty bread for mopping up all the delicious juices.

Serves 4

4 medium (approx. 450–500g) live lobsters

7 tablespoons olive oil

1 medium and 1 small onion, chopped

5 garlic cloves, 1 crushed, 3 sliced and 1 left whole

1 small carrot, chopped

1 celery stick, chopped

100ml brandy

100ml dry white wine

3 bay leaves

4 large thyme sprigs

1 large red pepper, deseeded and finely chopped

750g skinned, deseeded and chopped vine-ripened tomatoes, fresh or canned

1 teaspoon caster sugar

2 tablespoons chopped flat-leaf parsley, plus extra to serve

4 slices of crusty white bread, 1cm thick

4 heaped teaspoons Allioli (see page 227)

sea salt and freshly ground black pepper

Put the live lobsters in the freezer for 1 hour to send them to sleep before cooking. Bring one or two large pans of water to the boil, adding 30g salt per litre of water. Add the lobsters, bring the water back to the boil and cook for 5 minutes. Remove them from the pan(s) and leave until cool enough to handle. Discard the water. Remove the claws and the tails from the lobsters. Cut each tail across into 3 pieces through the shell, break the claws in half at the joint and crack the shells of each piece to make it easier to remove the meat later on. Break open the heads and use a teaspoon to scoop out the tomalley (the grey-green liver), and any red coral from each piece and put them in the fridge. Now break the heads and the legs into smaller pieces and reserve the cracked shells.

Heat 2 tablespoons of the olive oil in a large saucepan. Add the small chopped onion, the crushed garlic clove, the carrot and the celery and fry briskly for 5–6 minutes until soft and lightly golden. Add the pieces of lobster shell and fry for 2–3 minutes more. Pour over the brandy, set it alight and shake the pan until the flames have died down. Add the white wine and cook until it has almost disappeared, then pour over 1.2 litres water, add the bay leaves and thyme stalks (reserve the leaves) and bring to the boil. Cover and simmer for 30 minutes, then strain through a sieve into a clean pan. Discard the vegetables and shells. Boil the stock rapidly until it has reduced to 600ml.

For the stew, heat a further 3 tablespoons of the oil in a large casserole over a medium heat. Add the large chopped onion, the 3 sliced garlic cloves and the red pepper, cover and cook for 5 minutes until soft. Add the tomatoes, reserved thyme leaves, sugar and a little salt, bring to the boil and simmer uncovered for 20 minutes.

Meanwhile, use a pestle and mortar (or a mini food processor) to pound together the remaining whole garlic clove, the parsley, the remaining oil, the reserved tomalley and any coral into a smooth paste. Set aside.

Transfer the tomato sauce to a liquidiser and blend until smooth. Return it to the casserole with the stock, season and bring back to a simmer. Add the lobster pieces and simmer gently for 2 minutes. Stir in the parsley, garlic and tomalley paste and simmer for 1 minute. Meanwhile, toast the bread and spread each slice with a heaped teaspoon of the allioli. Put the toasts into the bottom of 4 large soup plates. Ladle the lobster and sauce into each bowl and serve sprinkled with parsley.

Chicken, avocado and melting cheese quesadillas

When you read this recipe, you may think that we're in Mexico, but you will find *quesadillas* throughout the Islands. I've included it because it's a tasty, fresh and easy dish to cook for guests when you haven't got much time.

Serves 4

8 teaspoons extra virgin olive oil

8 x 18cm soft flour tortillas (see page 229)

1 small cooked chicken, skinned, boned and shredded

1 large avocado, halved, skinned, stoned and thinly sliced

4 pickled green chillies, drained and thinly sliced

200g Mahón cheese (or mature Cheddar), coarsely grated

1 lime, halved

4 heaped tablespoons soured cream

sea salt flakes

For the tomato salsa

200g vine-ripened tomatoes, skinned, deseeded and finely chopped

1 green chilli, finely chopped

1 large garlic clove, finely chopped

6 spring onions, thinly sliced

10g coriander, chopped

Mix the ingredients for the salsa in a bowl and season to taste with salt. Heat a non-stick frying pan over a medium heat. Add 1 teaspoon of the oil, swirl it around and then place one tortilla in the base of the pan. Spread with one quarter of the tomato salsa, then scatter over a quarter (approx. 100g) of the chicken, a quarter of the avocado and 1 pickled chilli. Season with a little salt, then sprinkle over a quarter (approx. 50g) of the grated cheese and a squeeze of lime juice and dot with 1 heaped tablespoon of the soured cream. Place another tortilla on top and gently press down. This should take you about 2 minutes, by which time the bottom tortilla should be crisp and golden brown. Carefully slide it out onto a plate, add another teaspoon of oil to the pan and then invert the tortilla sandwich back into the pan and cook for another 2 minutes. Slide the *quesadilla* onto a board, cut into 6 wedges and serve hot, before cooking the next one in the same way.

Tortilla soup with choricero peppers, roasted green chillies and lime

This is an excellent soup with overtones from the New World, incorporating local ingredients, which is ideal for using up any leftover, stale corn tortillas. It is spicy and fresh at the same time and a comfort food. You can always change the ingredients to make use of any leftovers you have.

Serves 4

40g dried choricero peppers

6–7 tablespoons extra virgin olive oil

2 fat garlic cloves, halved

2 medium-hot green chillies, halved and deseeded

200g skinned, chopped vine-ripened tomatoes, fresh or canned

1 medium onion, halved and thinly sliced

1 teaspoon crushed dried chillies

1.5 litres homemade chicken stock

6 x day-old corn tortillas (see page 229)

200g cooked chicken, skinned and shredded

225g young Swiss chard, shredded, or baby spinach leaves

juice of 1 large lime (approx. 2 tablespoons)

20g coriander, roughly chopped

100g Spanish cheese, such as Manchego or Idiazabel, coarsely grated, to serve

sea salt flakes

Slit open the choricero peppers and remove and discard the stalks and seeds. Tear each one into 4 wide flat strips. Heat a dry frying pan over a medium heat, add the strips of dried pepper, skin-side down, and toast them for a few seconds until they darken slightly. Transfer them to a bowl, cover with boiling water and leave them to soak for 30 minutes.

Meanwhile, add 1 teaspoon of the oil to the frying pan, add the halved garlic cloves and fry gently until golden brown. Remove to a plate, add the green chillies and fry gently for 3–4 minutes until soft and lightly coloured. Set aside with the garlic. Drain the soaked peppers and scrape the flesh away from the skins. Discard the skins. Put the fried garlic cloves, green chillies, tomatoes and choricero pepper flesh into a mini food processor and blend to a smooth paste.

Heat 2 tablespoons of the oil in a medium pan. Add the onion and crushed dried chillies, cover and fry gently for 6–8 minutes until the onion is soft and lightly golden. Add the garlic and tomato paste to the fried onion and fry for 5 minutes until the mixture thickens. Add the chicken stock, bring to the boil and leave to simmer, uncovered, for 30 minutes.

Meanwhile, cut the corn tortillas into 5mm-wide strips. Heat the remaining oil in a frying pan, add one-third of the tortilla strips and fry until crisp and lightly golden. Set aside to drain on kitchen paper while you cook the remainder.

To finish the dish, stir the chicken and Swiss chard or spinach into the soup and simmer for 2 minutes. Stir in the lime juice, coriander and some salt to taste. Ladle into bowls, sprinkle with the fried tortilla strips and grated cheese and serve.

Spiced chicken and tomato sauté

This is a simple everyday supper dish, spiced up with flavours from the Americas, which I like to serve with steamed rice. I never used that many spices until I came to London and started working with David Eyre, and it has inspired me to adapt so many classical Spanish dishes to give them my own twist.

Serves 4

4 tablespoons olive oil

1 x 1.5kg chicken, jointed into 8 pieces

1 medium onion, finely chopped

4 garlic cloves, crushed

2 jalapeño (medium–hot green) chillies, deseeded and finely chopped

1 teaspoon sweet *pimentón*

1½ teaspoons ground cumin

8cm cinnamon stick

8 cloves

1 tablespoon chopped oregano

500g skinned, chopped tomatoes, fresh or canned

2 tablespoons tomato purée

150ml chicken stock

2 tablespoons lemon juice

50g raisins

50g pitted green olives, finely chopped

3 tablespoons chopped coriander

sea salt and freshly ground black pepper

1 hard-boiled egg, coarsely chopped, to garnish

steamed rice, to serve

Heat the oil in a large deep sauté pan. Season the chicken pieces well with salt and pepper and fry over a medium heat until richly golden all over. Lift the pieces of chicken onto a plate and pour off all but 2 tablespoons of the fat.

Add the onion, garlic and chillies to the pan and fry for 5 minutes until soft. Add the *pimentón*, cumin, cinnamon stick, cloves and oregano and cook for a further 1 minute. Stir in the tomatoes, tomato purée, chicken stock, lemon juice, raisins and half the olives and leave to simmer for 5 minutes.

Return the chicken pieces to the pan, spoon over some of the sauce, cover and simmer for 15–20 minutes until the chicken is cooked through and the sauce has reduced and slightly thickened.

Stir in the chopped coriander and adjust the seasoning to taste. Scatter over the rest of the olives and the hard-boiled egg and serve with steamed rice.

Chargrilled rabbit with spicy red and avocado green mojos

You must do this recipe once in your life. Try to buy wild rabbit if you can because the sauces can cope with the flavour, but feel free to use these sauces for chicken, lamb or any barbecued meat. Once again, you can see the Latin American influences in the *mojos*. Your guests will love them.

Serves 4

2 x 1.5kg wild or farmed rabbits

3 garlic cloves

6 tablespoons extra virgin olive oil

juice of 1 lemon (approx. 3 tablespoons)

1 teaspoon dried oregano

leaves from 2 x 12cm rosemary sprigs, finely chopped

2 teaspoons fennel seeds, crushed

sea salt flakes and freshly ground black pepper

patatas fritas, to serve (see page 117)

For the spicy red mojo

3 dried red choricero peppers

1½ tablespoons sherry vinegar

4½ tablespoons extra virgin olive oil

pinch of caster sugar

3 garlic cloves

¾ teaspoon sweet *pimentón*

¾ teaspoon crushed dried chillies

1 teaspoon freshly ground cumin seeds

For the avocado green mojo

3 tablespoons sherry vinegar

140ml extra virgin olive oil

pinch of caster sugar

6 garlic cloves

½ teaspoon crushed dried chilli flakes

1 ripe avocado, skinned, stoned and roughly chopped

½ teaspoon freshly ground cumin seeds

40g coriander leaves

Joint the rabbits according to the instructions on page 215, but cutting each saddle into 3 pieces and leaving the hind legs whole.

Crush the garlic cloves on a board under the blade of a large knife, sprinkle with a little salt and then work into a paste with the blade. Put the paste into a large shallow baking dish and mix in the oil, lemon juice, oregano, rosemary, fennel seeds and plenty of freshly ground black pepper. Add the rabbit pieces and mix well together. Cover, refrigerate and leave to marinate for 4–12 hours, turning the pieces every so often.

If you are using a charcoal barbecue, light it 30 minutes or so before you want to start cooking. When it is ready to cook on, the coals should be covered in a layer of light grey ash. If using a gas barbecue, light it 10 minutes beforehand.

Shortly before you are ready to cook the rabbit, make the *mojos*. For the spicy red *mojo*, slit open the choricero peppers and discard the stalks and seeds. Cover with boiling water and leave to soak for 30 minutes. Then drain, scrape the flesh away from the skins and discard the skins. Whisk the sherry vinegar with the olive oil, sugar and ½ teaspoon sea salt flakes. Put the red pepper flesh, garlic, *pimentón*, crushed dried chillies, cumin seeds and another ½ teaspoon sea salt into a mini food processor and blend to a smooth paste. Then, with the motor still running, gradually add the sherry vinaigrette to make a smooth sauce.

For the avocado green *mojo*, whisk the sherry vinegar with the olive oil, sugar and ½ teaspoon sea salt flakes. Put the garlic, dried chilli flakes, avocado, cumin, coriander leaves and another ½ teaspoon sea salt flakes into a mini food processor and blend to a smooth paste. Then, with the motor still running, gradually add the sherry vinaigrette to make a smooth sauce. Season to taste with a little more salt if necessary.

Lift the rabbit pieces out of the marinade and shake off the excess. Place them onto the barbecue and cook for 6 minutes on each side for the smaller pieces, 7–8 minutes for the larger pieces of saddle and the hind legs, brushing them with some of the leftover marinade now and then, until they are golden brown and cooked through. Pile the pieces onto a warmed serving plate and serve with the spicy red and avocado green *mojos* and some *patatas fritas* (chips).

Rabbit salmorejo

This is a signature dish of the Canary Islands, in many ways not that dissimilar to an *escabeche*, and bears no relation to the thick tomato soup from Cordoba with the same name. Make sure you marinate your rabbit for at least 6 hours, but preferably 12 hours, so that the flavours have time to get right into the meat before you cook it. This is often served with *patatas fritas*, which I love, but because the sauce is quite liquid, I think it also goes extremely well with steamed rice.

Serves 4

1.5kg farmed rabbit

6 garlic cloves, crushed

1 tablespoon sweet *pimentón*

1 medium-hot red chilli, deseeded and finely chopped

6 tablespoons extra virgin olive oil

3 tablespoons red wine vinegar or sherry vinegar

200ml dry white wine

leaves from a 10cm rosemary sprig, finely chopped

leaves from 1 large thyme sprig

2 medium onions, cut into thin wedges

3 bay leaves

150ml chicken stock

5g bunch of flat-leaf parsley sprigs, roughly chopped

5g bunch coriander sprigs, roughly chopped

sea salt and freshly ground black pepper

patatas fritas (see page 117), roast potatoes or steamed rice, to serve

To joint the rabbits, cut off the heads and discard. Cut off the front legs and remove and discard the bony ends. Cut off the hind legs and chop them in half through the bone with a cleaver. Then trim away the belly flap from the body section with scissors and cut each saddle across into 4 pieces, leaving the kidneys in place. Put the jointed pieces in a large, shallow baking dish.

Crush the garlic into a paste with ½ teaspoon salt using a pestle and mortar. Add the *pimentón* and red chilli and continue to crush into a paste, then stir in 3 tablespoons of the olive oil, the vinegar and 1 teaspoon freshly ground black pepper. Pour the mixture over the rabbit with the wine, rosemary and thyme and mix well together. Cover and refrigerate for up to 24 hours, turning the pieces every so often.

The next day, lift the rabbit pieces out of the marinade, shake off as much of it as you can and then season them with a little more salt. Keep the marinade. Heat 2 tablespoons of the remaining oil in a large flameproof casserole and fry the rabbit pieces in batches until nicely browned all over. Lift onto a plate and set aside.

Add the remaining olive oil and the onions to the pan and fry them until they are soft and lightly golden. Return the rabbit pieces to the casserole and pour over the marinade, stock and bay leaves. Bring to a simmer, cover and cook, for 40 minutes or until the rabbit is tender.

Lift the bay leaves from the pan and discard. If you like a smoother sauce, lift the pieces of rabbit onto a plate, tip everything else left in the pan into a food processor and whizz until smooth. Return the mixture to the pan with the rabbit and reheat for 5 minutes. Transfer the rabbit onto a serving plate, spoon over the sauce, garnish with the parsley and coriander and serve with fried potatoes, roast potatoes or steamed rice.

Roulade with banana, rum and brown sugar cream

Branzo de gitano is the cake I always had for my birthday when I was young. It's a roulade covered with cream and stuffed with custard. It's lovely, but this recipe, that I made with leftover bananas, is just so good. The first time I made it I ate the whole thing! It's a good way to use over-ripe bananas.

Serves 8

melted butter, for greasing
125g plain flour, plus extra for dusting
4 large free-range eggs
100g caster sugar, plus 3 tablespoons
25g light soft brown sugar
2 tablespoons warm water
2 teaspoons vanilla extract

For the banana cream

3 small, ripe bananas (those marked with dark brown spots)
2 tablespoons light soft brown sugar
2 tablespoons dark rum
200ml double cream

Preheat the oven to 190°C/gas mark 5. Line a 25 x 38cm Swiss roll tin with greaseproof paper, brush it with melted butter and then dust it with flour and knock out the excess.

Whisk the eggs, 100g of the caster sugar and the light soft brown sugar together in a large mixing bowl until the mixture is very thick and moussy and leaves a trail behind on the surface when drizzled from the beaters. Whisk in the warm water and the vanilla extract. Sift over and gently fold in the flour, one third at a time.

Pour the mixture into the prepared tin and tilt it backwards and forwards so that it fills the corners and forms a thin, even layer. Bake for 12–15 minutes until the centre of the cake feels slightly spongy and the sides have shrunk away slightly from the sides of the tin.

Place a large sheet of greaseproof paper onto the work surface and sprinkle it with the remaining caster sugar. Turn out the Swiss roll onto this and remove the lining paper. Place a slightly damp tea towel over the sponge and leave it to cool for 30 minutes.

For the banana cream, peel the bananas, slice them into a bowl and crush them into a paste using the back of a fork. Mix the brown sugar and rum together until the sugar has dissolved. Whip the cream and, as it begins to thicken, add the rum mixture and continue beating until the cream forms soft peaks. Fold in the crushed bananas.

Using a sharp knife, trim away the crisp edges from each long side of the sponge, then score a line 2.5cm in from one long edge. Spread over the banana cream. Then, starting with the scored edge nearest to you, firmly roll up the sponge.

To serve, cut the sponge across into 4 even-sized pieces and then each piece on the diagonal into triangular-shaped pieces. Place the straight-cut side down onto each plate (so that the top cut face is the sloping one) and serve.

Pan-fried bananas with brandy and orange butter

Please use medium-ripe bananas for this recipe. This is one of the first dishes I cooked when I was studying, but the orange butter is my adaption of the original dish.

Serves 4

300ml freshly squeezed orange juice (from approx. 4 oranges)

4 large ripe but firm bananas

45g butter

3 tablespoons light muscovado sugar

1 tablespoon brandy

1 tablespoon water

large pinch of salt

chilled coconut cream, to serve

Put the orange juice into a small pan and simmer vigorously until reduced to 50ml.

Peel the bananas and cut in half across, then cut each piece in half lengthways. Heat a large non-stick frying pan over a medium-high heat. Add 30g of the butter and leave until it has melted and turned nutty-brown. Add the banana pieces and sauté them for 1 minute, turning over halfway through, until lightly browned and just tender. Add 1 tablespoon of the sugar and shake the pan gently until the sugar has dissolved, then lift the bananas into 4 warmed shallow serving bowls.

Add the remaining sugar, the reduced orange juice, brandy, water, remaining butter and salt to the pan and simmer for 1 minute. Drizzle the sauce over the bananas and serve with the chilled coconut cream.

Pineapple, chilli, lime and mint served with pineapple and lime sorbet

This chilli and lime syrup has quite a kick to it, which I love, but do use just half a chilli if you prefer. One pineapple makes quite a lot of sorbet, but it keeps in the freezer for up to 3 months and is great to have as a standby. I love to add some cava to the sorbet for a nice refreshing drink after a long lunch in the sun...

Serves 6–8

1 large, really ripe and juicy pineapple

10 mint leaves, finely shredded, to serve

For the pineapple and lime sorbet

225g caster sugar

250ml water

6 juicy limes

1 tablespoon liquid glucose

1 large, really ripe and juicy pineapple

For the chilli and lime syrup

50g caster sugar

finely grated zest and juice 1 lime

½ –1 small (10g) medium-hot red chilli, deseeded and very finely chopped

For the sorbet, put the sugar and water into a pan and leave over a low heat until the sugar has dissolved. Then increase the heat slightly and simmer for 5 minutes. Meanwhile, finely zest and juice the limes. Remove the syrup from the heat and stir in the glucose syrup and lime zest. Leave to cool to room temperature, then stir in the lime juice.

Slice the top and bottom off the pineapple, sit it upright on a board and slice away the skin and all the little brown 'eyes'. Cut the fruit lengthways in half and remove the core with an apple corer. Roughly chop the flesh, put it into a food processor and blend until smooth. Strain in the lime-flavoured syrup and blend once more until smooth. Pour the mixture into a bowl, cover and chill overnight.

The next day, churn the sorbet mixture in an ice-cream maker. Alternatively, pour the mixture into a shallow plastic container, cover and freeze until firm but not rock hard. Scoop into a food processor and blend until smooth. Return to the container and freeze once again. Repeat the process 2–3 times more, then leave in the freezer until needed.

For the chilli and lime syrup, put the sugar and 50ml water into a small pan and leave to dissolve over a low heat. Bring to the boil and boil for 3 minutes, then remove from the heat and stir in the strained lime juice and chopped red chilli. Allow to become cold and then stir in the lime zest.

Prepare the second pineapple as before, then lay each piece cut-side down on a board and cut across into very thin slices. Slightly overlap these over the base of 6–8 dessert plates. Cover and chill until needed.

Just before serving, remove the sorbet from the freezer and allow it to soften slightly at room temperature for 15–20 minutes. Drizzle the chilli and lime syrup over the pineapple and sprinkle with the shredded mint. Top with a scoop of the pineapple and lime sorbet and serve.

Caramelised pineapple in black pepper and star anise syrup

This is quite an unusual recipe, but I love it because the caramelised pineapple is like candy. It's a great dinner party dish.

Serves 4

1 large ripe pineapple

250g caster sugar

1 litre water

2 whole star anise

1 teaspoon freshly ground black pepper

Pineapple and Lime sorbet (see page 220) or vanilla ice cream, to serve

Slice the top and bottom off the pineapple, sit it upright on a board and slice away the skin and all the little brown 'eyes'. Then cut the fruit lengthways into quarters, slice away the hard core and cut each piece in half lengthways again and then each piece across into two.

Put 175g of the sugar and the water into a medium pan and slowly bring to the boil, stirring the sugar to dissolve it. Add the pineapple pieces, bring back to a simmer and cook gently for 15–20 minutes, depending on the ripeness of your pineapple, until tender but not too soft.

When the pineapple is cooked, carefully lift the pieces into a bowl. Return the syrup to the heat and boil rapidly until reduced to 500ml. Allow to cool, then pour through a sieve back over the pineapple, cover and chill overnight.

The next day lift the pineapple out of the syrup onto a baking tray. Pour the syrup into a pan and boil rapidly until reduced to 250ml. Add the star anise and simmer for 1 minute more. Remove from the heat, stir in the black pepper and leave to go cold.

To serve, pour any excess syrup away from the tray and then sprinkle the pineapple heavily with half the remaining sugar. Caramelise, ideally with a blowtorch, or under a very hot grill, until golden and bubbling. Turn the pieces over and repeat. Lift the pineapple onto dessert plates and spoon over a little coarsely ground black pepper and star anise syrup. Serve with pineapple and lime sorbet or vanilla ice cream.

Sticky date and stem ginger puddings with toffee sauce

I know you must be thinking this sounds like a very English, classic sticky toffee pudding, but I use the dates from the Islands and I just love this recipe. The longer I live in London, the more British cooking is having an influence on me!

Serves 8

50g butter, melted, plus extra for greasing

175g dates, chopped

75g stem ginger in syrup, finely chopped

1 heaped teaspoon bicarbonate of soda

1 teaspoon vanilla extract

250ml boiling water

175g light muscovado sugar

2 medium free-range eggs, beaten

175g self-raising flour

pouring cream, to serve

For the toffee sauce

300ml double cream

75g butter

175g light muscovado sugar

Preheat the oven to 180°C/gas mark 4. Lightly butter 8 individual 200ml non-stick pudding moulds and base-line with discs of greaseproof paper.

Mix the dates, stem ginger, bicarbonate of soda and vanilla extract in a bowl. Stir in the boiling water and leave to soften for 5 minutes. Tip the mixture into a food processor, add the butter and sugar and process briefly until the ingredients are finely chopped but not a purée. Tip the mixture into a bowl and stir in the eggs and flour.

Divide the mixture between the prepared moulds and bake for 20 minutes or until a skewer pushed into the centre of the puddings comes away clean.

Meanwhile, for the sauce, put the cream, butter and sugar into a small pan and leave over a low heat, stirring now and then until smooth.

When the puddings are cooked, run a knife around the outside of each one and turn them out onto warmed serving plates. Remove the discs of greaseproof paper if necessary and pour some of the toffee sauce over each pudding. Serve with extra sauce and pouring cream.

Almond and honey creams with lemon verbena peaches

This is my interpretation of the first time I tried almond and honey creams in a restaurant in Lanzarote and thanks to my memory, I can't remember the name! They were using bananas from the islands, caramelised, but I decided to use peaches instead as they go so well with the flavour of the almonds and give a refreshing and sophisticated feel to the dish.

Serves 6

2 teaspoons powdered gelatine

300ml double cream

100ml whole milk

6 tablespoons clear honey

200ml carton almond cream (or extra double cream)

1–2 drops pure almond extract (optional)

For the lemon verbena peaches

2 large, ripe and juicy peaches

2 teaspoons caster sugar

2 teaspoons finely chopped lemon verbena or lemon thyme leaves

2 teaspoons lemon juice

Put 2 tablespoons water into a very small pan, sprinkle over the gelatine and leave to soak for 5 minutes. Meanwhile, warm the double cream, milk and honey together in another small pan. Dissolve the gelatine over a low heat until clear, then stir into the cream with the almond cream and almond extract (if using).

Pour the mixture into 6 tall glass dessert tumblers, each of 150ml capacity. Cover with clingfilm and chill for at least 6 hours or until set.

Shortly before serving, peel the peaches (see page 176), halve them, remove the stones and cut the flesh into thin slices. Put them into a bowl with the sugar, lemon verbena or thyme and lemon juice and mix together gently. Leave at room temperature for 15–20 minutes.

Remove the almond creams from the fridge, spoon some of the peaches into each glass and serve.

BASIC RECIPES

Olive oil mayonnaise

Makes approx. 300ml

2 large free-range egg yolks,
   at room temperature

2 teaspoons lemon juice

1 teaspoon Dijon mustard

½ teaspoon sea salt flakes

150ml extra virgin olive oil

150ml sunflower oil

Put the egg yolks, lemon juice, mustard and sea salt into a mixing bowl and lightly blend together. Gradually whisk in the oils, a little at a time, until you have produced a thick and silky-smooth mayonnaise.

Allioli

Makes approx. 180ml

2 large free-range egg yolks,
   at room temperature

1 small garlic clove, finely chopped,
   or crushed to a paste with the salt

1 teaspoon lemon juice

¼ teaspoon fine sea salt

150ml extra virgin olive oil

Put the egg yolks into a mixing bowl with the garlic, lemon juice and salt. Whisk them together, then very gradually whisk in the olive oil until you have a glistening sauce with the consistency of soft butter. Cover and chill until needed.

BASIC RECIPES

Romesco sauce

Makes approx. 250ml

2 dried ñora peppers

250g vine-ripened tomatoes

2 tablespoons extra virgin olive oil

25g blanched almonds

25g hazelnuts, skinned

1 15g slice of crustless white bread

1 fat garlic clove

1½ teaspoons sherry vinegar

sea salt flakes and freshly ground
   black pepper

Slit open the dried peppers and discard the stalks and seeds. Cover with boiling water and leave to soak for 2 hours.

Preheat the grill to high. Halve the tomatoes and place them skin-side up on a lightly oiled baking tray. Grill for about 5 minutes until the skins are black and the flesh is cooked. Remove the skins, drop the tomatoes into a food processor and leave to cool.

Put the olive oil into a frying pan over a medium heat, add the almonds and hazelnuts and fry until golden brown. Remove with a slotted spoon to a plate and leave to cool. Add the slice of bread and the garlic to the pan and again fry until they are golden brown. Set aside with the nuts and leave to cool. Remove the pan from the heat.

Scrape the flesh from the soaked peppers with a spoon and discard the skins. Add the flesh to the food processor with the fried nuts, bread, garlic, sherry vinegar and any leftover oil from the frying pan. Blend, using the pulse button, into a coarse paste and then season to taste. This can be used straight away or will keep in the fridge for several days.

Flour tortillas

Makes 8 large or 12 small

350g plain flour, plus extra for dusting

2 teaspoons baking powder

1 teaspoon salt

100g chilled lard, cut into small pieces

200ml lukewarm water

Sift the flour, baking powder and salt into the bowl of a food processor, add the lard and whizz together briefly until the mixture looks like fine breadcrumbs. Tip the mixture into a bowl, stir in the warm water and mix together into a soft dough. Turn out onto a lightly floured surface and knead briefly until smooth. If making large tortillas, say for *quesadillas* (see page 208), cut the dough into 8 even-sized pieces. If you want smaller tortillas, cut the dough into 12 pieces. Roll each one into a ball between the palms of your hands. Put onto a plate, cover with a layer of clingfilm and leave to rest for 1 hour.

To cook the tortillas, heat a dry, heavy-based frying pan over a medium heat. Take one ball of dough and flatten it slightly in a little flour, first on one side and then the other, into a disc. Roll out thinly, giving it a slight turn now and then, into either a 17–18cm disc or a 10–12cm disc. Place the tortilla into the hot pan and cook for about 15–20 seconds until it is marked with dark spots, then turn over and cook for another 20 seconds. Flip it back over and cook for 10 seconds more, then flip one last time and cook for a further 10 seconds. Remove and wrap in a clean tea towel to keep warm while you cook the remainder in the same way.

Corn tortillas

These make a great wheat-free, gluten-free alternative to bread.

Makes 12

125g *masa harina* (Mexican maize flour)

180–200ml hot water

salt

Sift the *masa harina* and 1 teaspoon salt into a mixing bowl and gradually stir in enough hot water to make a slightly moist dough. Cover and set aside for 15 minutes. Then divide the dough into 12 even-sized (approx. 25g) pieces and roll them into balls. Working with one ball at a time, roll or press it out between 2 small squares of greaseproof paper or clingfilm into an 11–12cm disc.

To cook the tortillas, heat a dry, heavy-based frying pan over a medium heat. Peel the paper or clingfilm from one tortilla, add it to the pan and cook for about 45 seconds until lightly coloured with little brown spots. Flip it over and cook for another 45 seconds, by which time it should be puffing up and lightly browned on the underside. Wrap each tortilla in a clean tea towel as you cook it to keep it warm and stop it drying out. Cook the remainder in the same way.

SPANISH FLAVOURS: INDEX

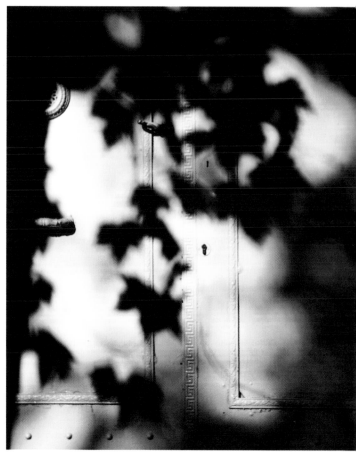

ACKNOWLEDGEMENTS

I want to say a huge thank you to my Mum and Dad – this book is dedicated to you.

And a big thank you to Debbie Major for helping me with the book. I had a lovely time testing and writing the recipes with you.

To my sister Isabel and my brother Antonio and sister-in-law Maria Jose; my nieces and nephews Carmen, Juan, Marina, Antonio and Cristina, for their great support and inspiration.

To Peter for his patience and help in tasting new recipes.

To Sophie Allen for your patience and help, to Kyle Cathie and all the team at Kyle Books.

To Emma Lee, for her friendship and for doing a wonderful job taking beautiful photographs for the book.

Gracias to Hannah Norris for her never-ending hard work.

To my agent Martine Carter for your help.

To Rick Stein for your support and all the team at Denhams TV, especially Arezoo for a great time filming in Spain.

To my business partners Herve, Gavin, Michael and Nialll for your confidence in my projects.

To Catriona for all her help with my website.

To all the staff and friends at 'José' and 'Pizarro' – too many to say names!

To all my neighbours and friends in Bermondsey Street for making me feel at home.

And to all the British and Spanish press for their support!